Whittling for Beginners Handbook

Starter Guide with
Easy Projects, Step by Step Instructions and Frequently Asked Questions (FAQs)

Stephen Fleming

© Copyright 2020 - All rights reserved.

The content contained within this book may not be reproduced, duplicated, or transmitted without direct written permission from the author or the publisher.

Under no circumstances will any blame or legal responsibility be held against the publisher, or author, for any damages, reparation, or monetary loss due to the information contained within this book. Either directly or indirectly.

Legal Notice:

This book is copyright protected. This book is only for personal use. You cannot amend, distribute, sell, use, quote or paraphrase any part, or the content within this book, without the consent of the author or publisher.

Disclaimer Notice:

Please note the information contained within this document is for educational and entertainment purposes only. All effort has been executed to present accurate, up to date, and reliable, complete information. No warranties of any kind are declared or implied. Readers acknowledge that the author is not engaging in the rendering of legal, financial, medical, or professional advice. The content within this book has been derived from various sources. Please consult a licensed professional before attempting any techniques outlined in this book.

By reading this document, the reader agrees that under no circumstances are the author responsible for any losses, direct or indirect, which are incurred as a result of the use of the information contained within this document, including, but not limited to, —errors, omissions, or inaccuracies.

Bonus Booklet- DIY Series

Thanks for purchasing the book. In addition to the content, we are also providing an additional booklet consisting of Monthly planner and Project Schedule template for your initial projects.

Also, it has a few evergreen whittling patterns for your practice.

Download the booklet by typing the below link.

(* Note: This booklet is common for wood and leather crafts)

http://bit.ly/leatherbonus

Cheers!

Copyright © 2020 Stephen Fleming

All rights reserved.

Table of Contents

PREFACE

I'm excited to release my third book in the DIY series, and I must say I'm truly enjoying the journey. I've been practicing these arts, along with my wife, for the last five years.

My wife has introduced me to the world of Whittling. It has been an incredible journey for the last few years while she's mostly focusing on Whittling and Wood Carving projects, and I'm supporting her all the way.

I've been working alongside her and learning the craft. As I was already into Leathercraft and Pyrography, I acquired the basics quickly. But reaching the intermediate level in any art requires practice and patience.

In sum, I'm trying to take you from point A to B in your whittling journey. After reading this book; you'll be able to reach point B, where you can:

- Appreciate the art
- Understand the basics of tools and concepts
- Get answers to beginner level frequently asked questions
- Complete your first project

And above all, you'll start feeling like an insider in the craft and make a strong connection. You'll then begin looking for wood crafts around you and observe the craft items you were ignoring or walking by earlier.

I've included realistic photographs, discussions, tips which I've received during my journey in Whittling over the years.

One of the old practitioners told me once; **"Whittling for me is more than just an art. It is like meditation and rather therapeutic. Every single time you create something, it brings you the delight and also the happiness that meets your mind and soul."**

Cheers, and let's start the journey.

Stephen Fleming

1.Decide what you want to do. "Everything" is too broad a category. Begin somewhere and also stick with it until you're ready to move to the next niche of Whittling.

2. If you aren't ready to invest cash, obtain your pocketknife and a piece of green scrap wood and also begin making method cuts: Stop cuts, scoop cuts, push cuts, and even pull cuts. Find out the various things you can do just with a knife.

3. When you make a decision to take the plunge and also open up your budget for tools, obtain a top-quality bench knife (for the large job) and a good quality detail knife. Acquire something decent, so you can buy it as soon as (Helvie's, Drake's are what I like). Flexcut's are common and also of good quality.

4. Get a good Kevlar glove for your other hand. Kevlar will certainly make the difference between a trip to the medication cupboard for a Band-Aid, and also a trip to the hospital for stitches. Don't consume alcohol and carve; surgical treatment is pricey!

5 Take a class if you can: "I intended to Make my own errors." I suggest you to desert this line of reasoning. YouTube works far better AFTER you've done some hands-on. Typically the regional carving clubs in your area are a good place to start your journey and familiarize yourself with the process.

6. Together with point # 5, many courses/classes will certainly have a collection of tools you require for the class. I've actually learned that this is a terrific place to start with purchasing tools. As you discover over time, you can add to the core group of tools, as needed.

7. Spending plan: It's been a while because I acquired my stuff, but I believe a good ballpark to get going is around $300 ish. Over time you can boost your tools. I'd certainly deny anything based on the reasoning, "Oh I want to do it someday," since you'll end up with a drawer full of tools you never use. The same applies to the more customized tools like Skew chisels, or scorps. They are helpful, yet you virtually never use them in the initial phase.

8. Find out how to sharpen your tools. There are numerous ways to do it, find one that works well, and stay with it. You'll likely spoil several tools throughout that "training" period. Treat this as a learning exercise.

9. Obtain the right kind of wood and remain with it. Basswood is where lots of people start, and it's popular for a good reason. Something I'd certainly suggest is if you obtain a piece of walnut or other wood, don't use your softwood tools on it.

10. Power tools: If you're likely to purchase power tools, one of the most beneficial power tools I have is my bandsaw.

1. Introduction to Whittling

The first question I had while starting Whittling was," **Is Wood Carving and Whittling the same?"**

So below is the answer as per Wikipedia and other sources:

- Occasionally the terms **"Whittling"** and **"Carving"** are made use of interchangeably, but they denote various arts.
- Carving employs making use of chisels, cuts, with or without a mallet, while whittling entails only making use of a knife.
- Carving also involves powered equipment such as lathes.

Wood Working with Lathe and other Tools

Whittling with aKnife

Woodcarving enthusiasts comprehend the difference between carving and whittling; however, somebody without any knowledge of the topic may not understand the distinction. Carving involves using a knife, a chisel, and also a club to develop a figure or sculpture; whittling is easier than carving because it involves only a knife and wooden piece to make artistic creations.

Whittling varies from shaving the tip of a tree branch to transforming a block of wood into a plaything watercraft. Many woodcarvers slam whittling as an amateurish hobby that just old men do to 'whittle away their time.' Nonetheless, whittling can create impressive outcomes like the wooden mallard duck decoys that interest the general public.

Wooden Mallard Duck

Examples of Whittling

Pic Credit: GWphotograph [CC BY-SA (https://creativecommons.org/licenses/by-sa/4.0)]

File URL: https://upload.wikimedia.org/wikipedia/commons/f/fe/Examples_of_Whittling.jpg

Cultural Views on Both Crafts

There are conflicting views of the woodworking field over the distinction between carving and whittling. Some suggest that carving is more of a European woodworking method, and whittling is an American leisure activity.

Serious woodcarvers would probably not like being called whittlers since whittlers utilize a knife to shave off timber from a stick.

One difference between carving as well as whittling might be the woodworking tools used by professionals. Some sources suggest that whittling includes knife jobs, which implies the woodworker makes use of merely a knife to make the final woodcraft. Only producing a tip on a stick would certainly be deemed as whittling in specific woodworking circles.

On the other hand, carving might involve making use of several woodworking devices to remove excess material, such as gouges, files as well as specialized blades. Carvers discover different woodworking techniques to derive the most to take advantage of a range of tools. While carvers frequently perform the very same blade job as whittlers, some consider making use of new devices as a significant distinction in between carving as well as whittling.

Some recommend there's no real difference between carving and whittling, besides the woodworker's personal preference. An American woodworker might describe himself or herself as a whittler for no other factor than that's the traditional name of the profession. A French woodworker may refer to himself or herself as a carver for the same conventional reason. There are numerous subcategories in woodworking, so a craftsman calls himself or herself a "chip carver" or an "ornamental woodcarver" according to his/her personal woodworking interests.

Purists think about whittling to be more of a pastime and carving to be more of a profession. The legendary image of older guys resting outside a general store and also whittling shavings from sticks tend to place whittling in a separate group than of vintage carvers skillfully developing elaborate designs on an expensive piece of timber furnishings. Whether this distinction between carving and whittling is fair and remains a major point of disagreement. However, wood carving tends to be viewed as a more advanced craft than wood whittling.

History of Whittling

Wood Carving is probably among the oldest kinds of art that originated when a human formed an item of wood with a sharp rock.

Man Whittling

Pic Credit: State Library and Archives of Florida [Public domain]

File URL: https://upload.wikimedia.org/wikipedia/commons/c/ce/Man_Whittling-_Sarasota%2C_Florida_%288147479321%29.jpg

Whittling developed when honed metal knives were used to carve a handheld piece of wood, making it one of the earliest kinds of carving.

Whittling is a form of sculpting that's done typically by utilizing nothing more than a knife. And also, a perfectionist would say that whittling is done by using nothing more than a "pocket" knife. Whittling is an American term which, as I stated above, means to sculpt making use of a knife. It's a subcategory of woodcarving. In other places worldwide, if you were to carve utilizing a knife, it would be described as woodcarving.

The history of whittling truly begins in early America, where smart folks could whittle just about anything, anywhere. Throughout the early years, a Swiss army knife was economical, maybe quickly as well as securely brought, and also perhaps conveniently developed. And also, suitable softwood was easily bountiful, mostly pine or willow at that time.

The Whittling Boy Painting: Winslow Homer / Public domain

Whittling, nonetheless, didn't become a widespread leisure activity in the United States until the Civil Battle in 1865 when soldiers with skilled hands whittled for hours to pass the time. Whittling became a preferred pastime of soldiers across ranks. Some soldiers that had the routine of carrying around folding jack knives became efficient whittlers. They turned wood right into strolling sticks, figurines, sculptures, smoking cigarettes pipelines, followers, whistles, and also a ball in a cage. After the battle, these same guys taught soldiers, especially in the Indian and Spanish-American wars, exactly how to whittle.

Some of the Civil War veterans ended up being migrants as well as employees that worked with railways, ranches, and building roads. Anywhere they went for work, migrant farm laborers, also called 'Hoe kids,' or 'Hobos,' carried their hoes with them to grow plants. Many things they made from whittling were exchanged for food, clothing, and shelter.

The art of whittling continued after the Great Depression, which made kids proceed to make things with their pocket knives. After the Second World War, the G.I. Bill enabled veterans to get a university education to obtain work in industries like production and construction. Subsequently, whittling started to shed its ground as a sought after skill. Nevertheless, the Boy Scouts incorporated whittling as one of the skills members required to practice in the 1950s. The Boy Scouts also funded whittling competitions.

The art of whittling declined in 1965 with the arrival of the digital age when customers changed their focus to home entertainment instead of hands-on tasks. Additionally, the public institutions ceased its industrial as well as hands-on courses, limiting direct exposure for students that may have developed an interest in these skills.

Woodcarving grew a little in the mid-1970s with the increase of woodcarving clubs showing up here and there across the country. Many of these subscription organizations sponsored Woodcarving workshops that showed the essential skillsets. Woodcarving fanatics attempted to preserve a rise in whittling passion, yet until now, they've generated minimal results from more youthful generations.

After the 1980s and the development of the first video games, youngsters were mostly engaged online. Utilizing the hands was more regarding in the form of manipulating a joystick or computer game controller to developing something from square one. From Ataris to Playstations to Xboxes, as well as currently virtual reality, youths are more engaged in digital hobbies rather than old school ones like whittling.

WhittlingNow

Recently, non-electronic arts, as well as crafts, have been organizing substantial returns as people (consisting of young people) look for methods to take a break from all the computer screens and also smartphones.

These crafts were historically gender-specific, for example, whittling for gents and knitting for ladies. But with the revival of these art forms, in recent years, have made these crafts gender-neutral. Nowadays, in the whittling community, you can find many ladies of all age groups, and similarly, in the knitting community, you can find men.

Whittling is achieving revived interest across genders and geographies with many new whittling clubs outside the US in countries like the UK.

Supporters of the modern whittling state that it's a terrific remedy to the stress of modern-day life and a type of digital detox. It's now generating interest across genders, age groups, and geographies.

Hobby and Recreation

The very first point concerning whittling is that it's for recreation and leisure. Here you create something with your hands, and that's hugely satisfying.

Developing something via your hands is healing and also reflective. It's energetic and, consequently, favorable to your well-being.

Many people got to a bar to relax and unwind after a day or week of work. This hobby is portable and low cost and helps you unwind from your daily activities.

 All you need is a pocketknife and also a piece of wood, and you're prepared to go.

The crux is:

"The difference between Whittling and Woodcarving is to do with the mind frame." In carving, you're settling up the job in a goal-oriented manner with preparation as well as criteria of implementation in mind. In contrast, with whittling, you take one day at a time and allow spontaneity to take control of the project.

One more analogy is: *Whittling is like an unplanned vacation (go with the flow), and Wood Craving is like planning a vacation through a tour operator!*

Tips for Whittling Wood

Whittling wood has been a pastime since sticks were lying to be sharpened by some tools. Whittling has been passed down from one generation to another for centuries. And also, the fantastic feature about it is that there's a minimal financial investment needed to start.

- **The Wood**

The simplest method to start whittling wood is to discover a stick or piece of wood and start slicing away. If you intend to begin with pre-cut timber, acquire blocks and softwood sticks.

One of the most usual types of whittling timber is basswood. It's soft and has a marginal grain to manage. Other right wood kinds include pine as well as cedar. Wood blocks can be valuable in sanding your work as well.

- **A Simple Pocketknife**

The most basic blade to utilize for whittling is a pocketknife. It's easy to keep and also has other functions, as well. Plus, unlike specialty knives, pocket knives can be discovered virtually anywhere. Pocket knives with various blades can offer you a variety of cuts.

Pocket Knife

- **A Carving Blade**

A cost-effective, sculpting knife can be purchased online. It may be handmade by a craftsman using a part of a straight razor. Blades have a larger handle for more control and also typically stay sharper longer. They likewise are, generally, less complicated to sharpen and are better at the detailed job, like feathers as well as beaks. Just take care because these are fixed blades. You might intend to think about placing an old white wine cork on end as protection.

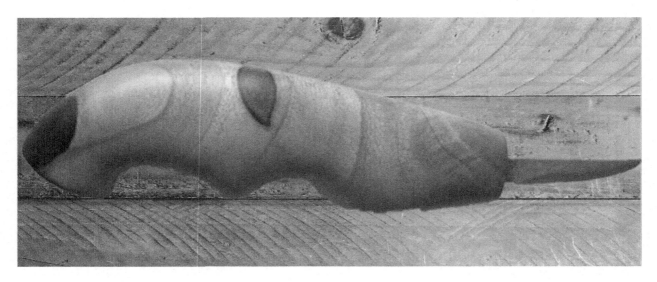

Carving Knife

- **Spoon Carving Knives**

As with any pastime, whittling wood can come with a range of gears. This blade is a unique knife that is useful when whittling spoons. The bent blade aids cut the dish of spoons as well as ladles. It's harder to hone then straight knives yet finishes curved cuts.

If you intend to try spoons and also ladles, try fruit-tree woods like apple or pear.

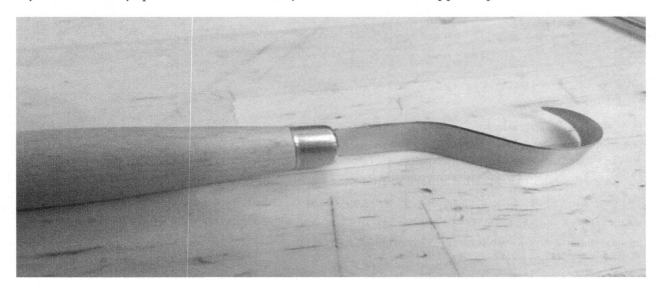

Spoon Carving Knife

- **A dull knife cuts you quicker.**

An old saying is that a dull blade cuts you quicker than a sharp one. The idea is counter-intuitive initially, yet belongs to the force required to cut. The tougher you have to press or pull to eliminate the excess timber, the higher the power the blade may strike you with if it slides. When you discover the cut getting harder, quit and sharpen the blade.

- **Strop or Rock**

You have to sharpen the blade while whittling timber. It can undoubtedly be individual preference, but there are two basic camps, strops or stone. Usually, those utilizing a pocketknife use a stone, while those using a carving blade will use a leather strop, revealed right here. You can make your very own strop by gluing part of a belt to a piece of timber. Draw the blade backward and forward numerous times at a low angle (10 to 20 levels).

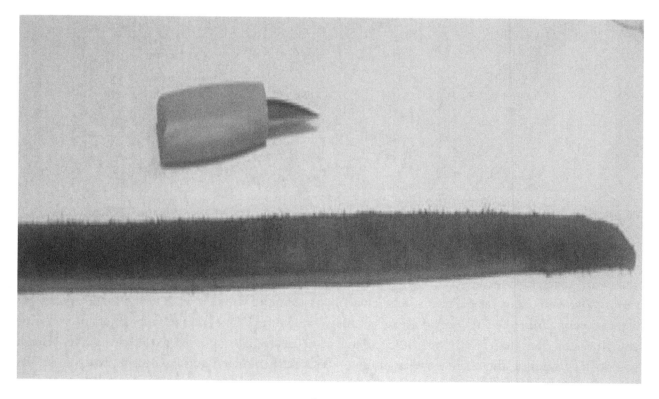

Strop

- **The Cuts**

You can cut away from on yourself, and of course, this is generally a good guideline. Nonetheless, when trimming wood, several cuts require you to cut toward yourself. The pushing cut takes off big pieces. The thumb-push utilizes the other hand's thumb to guide the blade as you reduced. The whittling cuts, like if you're whittling apples, is a pulling cut that cuts towards you and your thumb. It can take a bit of technique to obtain these cuts right.

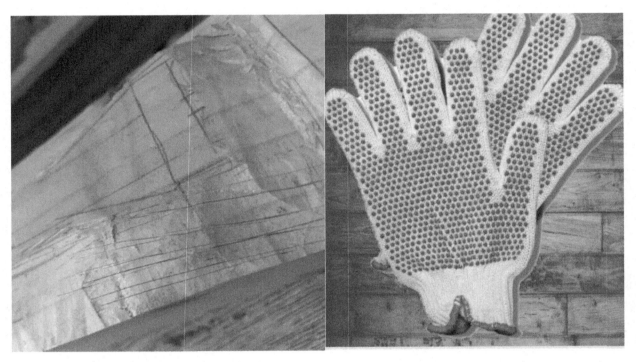

Cut   Gloves

- **To Glove or Otherwise**

There are several gloves around to secure you while whittling wood. Among my favorites is a cut-proof glove with a Kevlar palm. It's quite challenging to injure yourself while using one of these. It's likewise very hard to feel the wood as well as adjust the knife. I've seen many old-timers not wearing any gloves as they didn't start with it, and later, it became challenging to work with gloves. But if you've been wearing them since the beginning, you'll get habituated and believe me that's a worthy habit to make!

Few Tips from Experts

- Make sure the wood you are utilizing is dry. Wet wood can warp or fracture when dried out.

- If you're having a problem achieving great detail because your wood is hard, then try using a 50/50 mix of alcohol and water.

- Consider using sculpting handwear/gloves to avoid injury. If you decline to wear gloves, think of wearing a thumb pad. If you don't intend to put on a thumb pad, at least shield your thumb under some layers of duct tape.

- Don't hurry. Make regulated cuts and also remove wood in thin layers or risk tearing the wood and leaving ugly marks behind.

- If you want to keep your hands free when whittling, use a device like a clamp or vice to attach the wood to a solid surface.

- Sharpen your knife on a regular basis. If you observe that it's an obstacle to making your cuts, it's most likely that your blade needs to be honed.

- Don't expect to master this skill overnight. Wood sculpting needs a lot of practice as well as perseverance. Good carving originates from experience as well as persistence. So don't get discouraged if whittling doesn't come to you as quickly as you seek. Continue working on your skills, and you would get there.

2. Wood for Whittling

Woods

Typically speaking, woods have three main properties that a carver will want to take into consideration:

- **Hardness**
- **Grain**
- **Shade or color**

Hardness relates to the wood's resistance to cutting or infiltration by a carver's tools. Technically, woods are categorized as either hardwoods or softwoods. Usually, softwoods are those with needles or leaves that are not lost in the winter months.

One exemption is larch. Larch does shed its needles as it's categorized as softwood. For example, softwoods include all the fruitwoods located in places around Chelan that are deciduous. Understand that, in some cases, these classifications can be deceiving because there are many softwoods harder than some hardwood and vice versa.

For example, one of my favorite types is-basswood, which is softer than Alaska Yellow Cedar, a true softwood. One needs to factor in hardness when considering a sculpting application.

For example, if you were carving a walking stick or walking cane, then you'd want hardwood for strength. Lots of softwoods don't have the required strength to make a walking stick.

There's a word of caution about working with saw /wood dust of these woods. Many unique kinds of wood, such as those from tropical regions, are harmful. Care should be taken while working by always using a face mask. Some carvers are also allergic to the touch of particular woods.

The grain is the visible strata or lines in the wood. The grain is commonly development rings, and in softwoods, the grain is usually big as softwood trees expand reasonably fast.

A carver usually carves with the grain adhering to the very same direction as the lengthiest measurement of the carving. You've all heard the term: **"that goes against my grain."** The phrase originates from the fact that carving against the grain is most difficult.

Typically, even if it's possible to sculpt against the grain, it'll undoubtedly wear and tear, leaving a rugged surface. I recall a wood artist telling his audience that the **wood will tell you if you carve in the wrong direction.** What he was describing was that if you carve against the grain, then you'll feel the resistance. Carving with the grain is usually smooth.

Color is necessary if you don't paint your project and also appreciate the natural wood. We do add oils and often stains to improve the appearance. We usually tend not to paint wood as it conceals the all-natural appeal found in wood.

Excellent woods with color are walnut and also butternut. Several others aren't always dark woods like Alder and also Desert Juniper t are reasonably attractive. There are some woods with creamy or light sapwood (outer wood) as well as a salmon or brownish inside (heartwood). These twin tone woods are fun to carve, and also one can be creative with carvings using the various colors. An instance is the wizard imagined right here with blonde hair and a natural complexion on the face. This item is Diamond Willow from Alaska, among my preferred woods.

One requires a selection of wood for a carving after evaluating the above.

Over the years, we've carved on many kinds of wood. We've also carved that pesky bitterbrush that grows around North Central Washington. Nevertheless, I do have my favorites. Let's point out a few of them here, and in the near term (future column), I'll discuss each of them more thoroughly, defining their features. A few of my favorites are:

- **Walnut**
- **Basswood**
- **Mahogany**
- **Yellow Cedar**
- **Desert Cedar**
- **Western White Pine**
- **Ruby Willow**

Carvers sometimes discover wood too difficult or perhaps too soft to carve. Woods can be hard for small detail knives, and also softwoods can easily be crushed when a knife isn't razor-sharp.

The suggested treatment for both of these is to spray the place to be carved with a high dosage of 50/50 massaging alcohol as well as water. The combination works magic in both situations, and also it dries without a trace. Give it a try!

Basswood On The Working Table

Which wood should I choose?

Here's the most common question wood crafters ask, **"Which wood do I choose for woodcarving?"**

Nevertheless, there are many times where we see a distinct piece of wood that gives us many ideas on what could be done on it.

It may have a twist, knot, or an apparent imperfection that's striking or creative.

As a true artist, stare at your piece and believe me, something would pop out as an idea to be carved on that piece. As famously cited that food has been created for everyone, and it would be delivered, similarly, **every wooden piece has its fate sealed, and that carving has to be done on it**!

Looking back, I can undoubtedly say that the whittling pieces which delighted me the most were those.

In looking back at the whittlings and also carvings that I've done, the ones that stand out the most are the ones that contain some remarkable and distinct features. The option is to resist doing anything with it until something does come to mind and also it will.

For cases where we have a project in mind or have been requested to create something particular, we should pick a suitable piece of wood.

So, let's discuss the procedure of selecting the wood for our job.

The Wood

There are thousands of woods in the world of ours, but I'll limit this discussion to a couple of woods used for woodcarving or the ones which are my favorites.

Also, let me point out here that the top quality of the wood is essential for creating an excellent whittling project.

For example, all basswood is not of the same quality. It is not enjoyable to carve a poor-quality piece of wood—use caution in buying wood online as you can't check it physically (I'm still old fashioned about buying wood!).

No discussion of wood would indeed be full without consisting of Basswood (Tilia Americana). These days, the wood of choice for newbie carvers is basswood.

While practically a hardwood, basswood is a softer wood and hard enough to hold incredible detail as it was fine, even grain.

It falls somewhere between pine as well as birch regarding the convenience of carving goes. One factor favored by caricature carvers is that it can be cut with a knife throughout grain conveniently.

That attribute is one-of-a-kind as compared to most woods.

Cutting cedar will likely result in squashing the wood, despite having a sharp blade. Plus, it's virtually impossible to cross gain on hardwoods as a result of their hardness.

Basswood isn't the most beautiful of woods, and also it has to be repainted if the last coating of your carving isn't blonde.

Regarding the final finishing, the wood surface can be sanded easily.

.

Bocote, rosewood, and zebrawood

Western White Pine/Idaho White Pine

The preferable kinds of wood for newbie whittlers as well as carvers include Western White Pine/Idaho White Pine.

One can attain some respectable detail with it with an extremely sharp knife and specifically by adding the above-referenced alcohol mix.

In the very early days of whittling in America, Western White Pine was the wood choice for whittling because it was plentiful, economical, or perhaps complimentary and was used for everything imaginable at the time. We hear that disease wiped out Western White Pine, and it's rather rare today.

An extremely appealing and much more affordable wood to carve is Butternut. I've heard it described as "the pauper's walnut." It is a beautiful wood by merely including a light oil finish and does not require either painting or discoloration. Also, this is the wood of choice by many experts.

Cherry is, in my opinion, the gorgeous wood on the marketplace. Nonetheless, it's tricky to carve with my hands. Similar to Butternut, only light, all-natural oil is required. As a result of Cherry's hardness, it's necessary to rough out a cherry task with a power cutter such as a Kutzall or Sabre Tooth burr and then end up with a gouge.

While possible, it's incredibly difficult to carve with a knife.

Birch is a white wood suitable for carving and also accomplishing great detail. It's more challenging than basswood but softer than maple and also most fruitwoods. Due to its all-natural white color, your final finish will either require entirely all-natural or repainted. My very own experience has shown that it doesn't tarnish well.

A wood that I like to whittle and also have carved for years is Diamond Willow. It's a fine-grained wood with a large, salmon tinted heartwood surrounded by luscious sapwood. Diamond Willow is made use of strolling sticks.

A unique feature of is the many diamond-shaped cankers that form along the shaft, typically around tiny branches. It's one of the best woods for whittling. The one downside is that it is hardly ever larger than 3-4 inches and more frequently even smaller sized. It's a wood that you'll certainly want to physically checkout before acquiring. I've seen a lot of trash offers for sale, even by trusted carving supply shops.

Other Woods

The fact is, one can carve in practically any kind of wood. Found wood is both fun to carve as well as extremely eye-catching. I suggest trying all the woods. I have a buddy, an experienced spoon carver, and he indulges in carving a wide choice of various woods all stunning. Like me, he resides in a fruit village where he collects trimmings from local fruit trees in the very early months of the year for his spoons.

Wood Grain

When I was struggling to understand the concept of wood grain initially, one old-time whittler told me, *"Think of the grain-like petting a cat. When you pet it head to tail, the fur all lies down, and the cat purrs. If you try to go from tail to head, it spikes up, and the cat gets very angry. Keep the cat happy."*

This analogy has stayed with me since then. Finally, let me discuss a couple of features of the wood grain. To begin with, wood grain is gorgeous, so don't be afraid of carving wood with a grain. As stated above, carving throughout grain frequently calls for using an alcohol mix, unless it's greenwood. Some years back, I heard a Native American carver inform a group of onlookers that the wood tells him, which way to carve. I initially thought, "What B.S." I found out later what he exactly meant. When one is carving and the blade "attacks" right into the wood, stop. Don't build on; it's time to quit. The resistance or attacking is telling you to stop and carve in the opposite direction. In the majority of woods, the grain doesn't run directly; it's frequently "ribbony," and a carver needs to take care of its direction before carving.

3. Tools

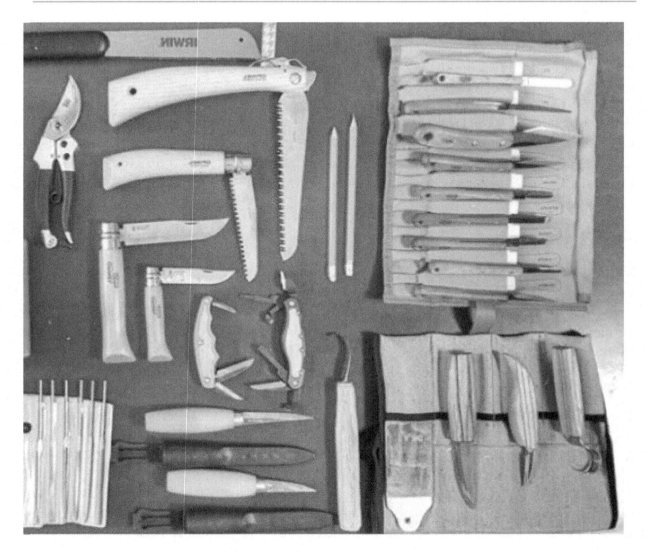

An Expert Woodcrafter's Tool Box

Believe it or not, you don't require a substantial collection of tools to be a master whittler. Some perfectionist carvers will undoubtedly tell you that using a dull pocketknife is the only real method to whittle, and also, they could not be wrong. A pocketknife is mobile and also offers a range of blade sizes, making them a great tool to carry with you.

Nevertheless, there are various other choices available out there. You can also work with whittling blades, since they don't fold but are great for detailed work. They're more durable than typical pocket knives, and also can have a curved blade. The curved edges give you much more comfort and are optimal for staying clear of discomfort and also tiredness throughout those lengthy whittling sessions. In case you're an experienced crafter trying to attain finer detail in your items, take into consideration buying a detailing knife. Whatever you're working with, bear in mind that the **sharpness of the tool is typically far more vital than the kind of tool**.

Which way to carve when working with grain:

Watch the Grains in Projects

The understanding of grain is essential to wood carving and where your intuition will establish in time. The orientation of the grain is most likely to figure out how quickly you can carve the wood. If you've ever before had a splinter, you understand what grain is as well as exactly how its orientation issues. You'll certainly wish to start with straight-grain wood (which is precisely what it seems like), where the grain runs in one direction. You can utilize the ends to establish what course the grain runs in. Keep in mind that the grain can go down a little. Standard vocabulary states: when carving parallel to the grain, you're carving with the grain. If carving opposite the direction of the grain, you're carving against the grain. If you're carving perpendicular to the grain, you're carving across the grain. You always wish to carve **with the grain or across the grain**. The best way is to make sure you're carving with the grain in the down direction.

All about Knives

Among one of the most crucial points in any leisure activity are the tools required. If you were a hunter, your gun, bow, and other tools are your best friends; and with years of experience, they become like an extended part of your body.

Suppose you were fishing after hunting, you now need to have the most efficient fishing devices suitable to your requirement. The only major device you would need for whittling is a knife.

Yes, you heard that right-- knives.

As you gain a lot more experience in this craft, you'll eventually develop a collection of knives. Also, you will certainly have your favorites, and also you'll ultimately wear off several of your knives by the time you become a master at whittling timber. However, don't stress over it-- think about them as your learning progresses.

More than Just a Tool

It doesn't matter just how or where you use your knife. Some do their whittling in the workshop, so that their devices and materials will certainly be within easy reach.

Nevertheless, you can also whittle at the fishing lake, awaiting the fish to be caught.

During these relatively idle and also dull times, you discover something exciting to whittle with your knife.

After gaining some experience, you'll definitely understand that the sharp object you have in your hand is more than a piece of metal. It's more than merely a device. It seems like an extension of your hand-- a part of your body.

Like every hobby, whatever it's you make with your knife should seem like pure joy as well, not a task. If the blade you're using doesn't feel comfortable in your hands after that, leave it.

The appearance and also the feeling of the blade will have an impact on your whittling abilities. Worst situation scenario-- you may cut your hand since the blade was as dull or it wasn't a great fit for your hand.

Pocket Knife vs. a Specialty Whittling Knife

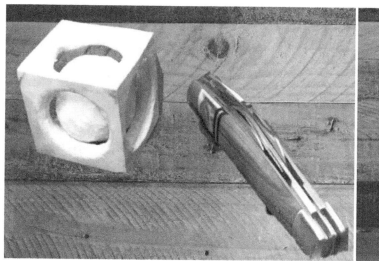

Pocket Knife

There's a little disagreement concerning which knife is the most effective whittler-- a specialized whittling knife or an antique pocket knife. Well, for purists, there's no other knife that works ideal for whittling other than the trusted pocket knife. For generations, individuals that have whittled many varieties of timbers and chips used nothing more than a hand pocketknife. You can say that the pocket knife has formed artworks that are no less than ruggedly good-looking. No doubt, you'll certainly experience those who will tell you that the only appropriate blade for true blue whittling is none other than a pocket knife. A pocket knife is an excellent choice because it is incredibly mobile.

You could be walking in a camping area someday and come across a great item of wood to work with merely resting on the ground out there.

You can take it back to camp, sit on a log, and also whip out your trusty pocket knife as well as start working. And that's practically the joy of this art. There's an additional advantage that a pocket knife can provide you that you won't get out of a specialized whittling blade, which is the fact that you already have greater than one type of knife available with the pocket knife.

Pocket knives can have several types of blades. For instance, if you require some intricate work, then you can take out the smaller sized knife; and if you need to carve the bowl of a wooden spoon that you're working with, you can pull out the rounded blade to remove more material.

Also, if you require removing larger pieces of timber and even material, then you can simply take out

29

the bigger blade to do just that.

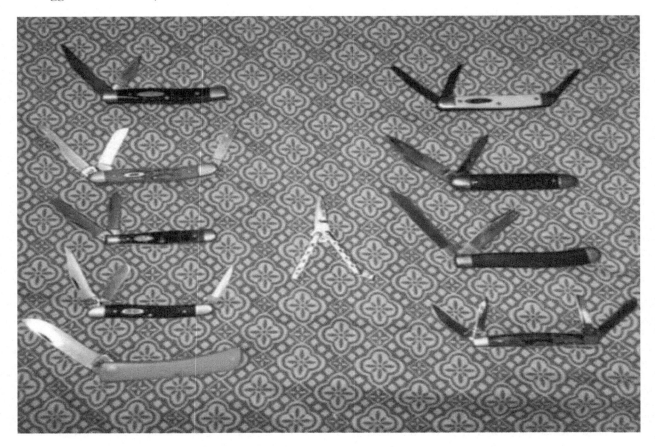

Collection of Pocket Knives

Why choose specialty whittling knives?

Some would say that specialty whittling knives are just later innovations that glossy marketing professionals wish to shove right into everyone's faces. However, it can also be argued that individuals who made these specialized whittling knives are fellow crafters who felt that they needed to create the very best blades for their craft. And so, we have specialized trimming knives today with the efforts of fellow whittlers. They were made to make working on timber a lot more comfortable. If you ever attempt one, you'll certainly discover that these knives; in fact, they really feel much better in your hand. One apparent disadvantage, though, is the reality that these knives have fixed blades.

Unlike the trusty pocket knife, you might end up with several of these blades in your toolkit. In short, set blades indicate less mobility. Given that they don't fold after that, they have a little bit of a bigger footprint-- which means you'll require a larger container or toolkit to carry all your knives.

However, on the plus side, these specialty whittling blades supply you a better grasp with a great deal of toughness than what you usually feel out of an old folding knife. It makes your strokes a lot firmer than you generally do-- offering you much better control over each cut.

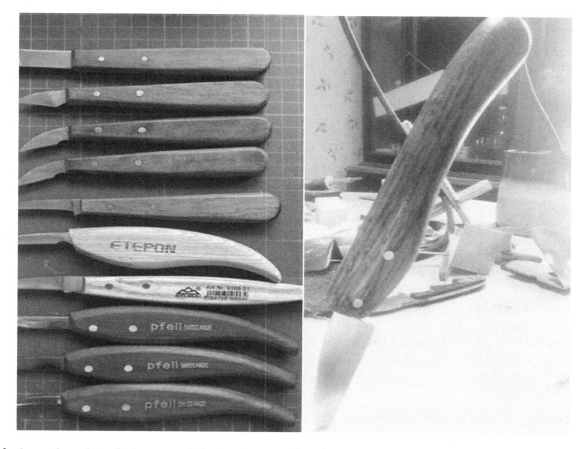

And given that they feel so much better in your hand, they likewise provide you another benefit. And that is, your hands will not feel too invested after a whittling session. You might even go at it longer with a specialty whittling knife since your hands won't burn out too quickly when you utilize them. These blades likewise hold a side reasonably perfectly, and that also makes them much more comfortable to hone. Some even have ergonomically developed handles, which do help reduce the level of tiredness you feel in your hands.

So, which knife should I use?

The solution to this universal question is that you need to have both types of knives. It's far better to have the very best of both types-- which is something that'll certainly assist you to understand the art of whittling. If you go to the house, then utilize your specialized knives, considering that you have your toolkit right there. However, if you take a trip or head out outdoor camping, then your pocketknife will certainly come in useful. In contrast, a collection of specialty trimming knives will just be irritating to bring along to the journey. Besides, as specified previously, at some point, you'll develop your collection of knives as you go ahead with your craft.

What I Like in a Knife

- Excellent quality high carbon steel
- A shorter blade, since I respect the fact that people can sculpt with long blades, but I prefer much shorter versions, and also I have much better control with a shorter blade.
- A knife with a slightly higher curvature, something similar to a clip blade. Also, a comfortable, sturdy handle.

What Makes a Great Whittler knife?

Now, whether you're making use of a specialty whittler knife or a folding pocketknife, you must understand what attributes to look for in a knife.

In this regard, you'll certainly likewise hear a lot of guidance, especially from old-timers who have gone to it a while. Now, collecting from that collective wisdom and, of course, from individual experience, here are several crucial points to try to find in a whittling knife.

First of all, you ought to seek a blade that has a genuinely steady geometry.

It'll allow better control as you change from one grip position to the following. You need to additionally favor a knife that does not have a lot of "belly" on it. When we claim "belly," we describe the rounded shape of the knife's edge.

What you need to be searching for is a blade that has a somewhat level as well as a straight cutting edge. Some knives have a sharp, rounded side-- you ought to stay away from those given that they're not as effective as knives that have a sharp straight side.

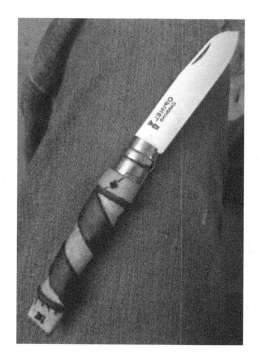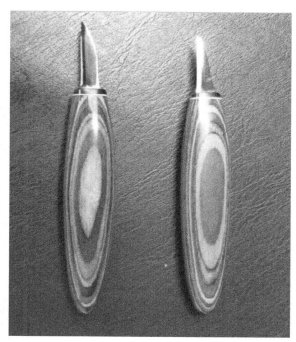

My Collection of Knives

Note that a lot of specialized whittling knives have this sort of edge. The type of steel used to make a knife can also be an aspect, but we'll get to that later.

In the meantime, you should understand that you don't intend to obtain a knife that's too tight or hard.

You don't desire that sort of knife because as you collaborate with a blade-like that the edge might chip off when the blade is too tough or as well rigid.

Get a knife that isn't too stiff. Bear in mind that the solidity of a knife has nothing to do with its durability and sturdiness. That suggests these knives can much better deal with pressures and also torsions specifically at the very end of the knife's blade.

Factors to Consider

Below are other aspects to take into consideration when you're buying a great whittling knife:

- **Blade Style**

The blade style is a significant element; nonetheless, it sometimes just comes down to individual choice. However, here's a general rule that you can pass; as long as feasible, you intend to have a flat blade surface running against the wood that you're collaborating with, the back of your blade should be strong. However, it should've been thick either. Once more, you want a knife that will be flexible as needed. That type of blade supplies a great deal of adaptability.

- **Type of Side**

You need to be aware that there are various sorts of edges, depending on the knife that you are considering. Some sides work better for timber carving than different other purposes. If you favor knives with a fixed blade, a Scandinavian or Scandi side will certainly be an excellent option. It's simple to hone as well as it gives you better control when you're doing your strokes.

Type of Steel

Now here's another vast subject and also there are certainly be enthusiasts and specialists who can discuss it all day. What I see right here is that good old tradeoff between two vital factors-- edge retention as well as solidity.

I prefer blades that can be curved to a particular level. A slightly bendy blade can have a couple of even more applications that you can't get out of a rigid blade. The sharpness of your knife converts to your very own safety and security.

Sharp blade, safety, and security? Yep, you listened to that right. Sure, it's sharp enough to carve an excellent pound of your flesh, but that's not the factor. If your blade is dull after that, it'll certainly tend to slip off the material that you are cutting or whittling. Simply put, the sharper the knife, the far better it can cut the timber as well as minimal opportunities that it will slip off as well as cut you. **Remember, on the planet of whittling; sharpness equates to safety.**

Should I obtain a carbon steel blade?

If you like to whittle with a pocketknife after that, you must know that a lot of these knives have blades made from stainless steel. Fixed bladed knives can be made from other kinds of steel. Keep in mind that stainless steel often tends to hold the side a lot longer contrasted to various types of steel. Well, for one point, it doesn't wear away. But there's a catch. Given that stainless steel dulls a lot longer, that means you'll certainly have to invest even more time sharpening it. Yep, there's continuously a tradeoff for everything.

Now, if you're into whittling with a fixed blade knife after that, you should know that most of them are made of high carbon steel. However, there are folding knives (i.e., pocketknife) that also have a high carbon blade. Knives that have this blade tend to be much more costly than the others. However, they are a great deal simpler to hone. You can sit down for a minute or two as well as hone your whittler knife in minutes. Their manufacturers incorporate the toughness of stainless steel along with the wonderful qualities of high carbon blades. You can call them hybrids-- and they can often be costly.

Location of Your Blade

Currently, this information is useful for pocketknives than anything else. Note that several of them have more than one knife or device included in the kit. The more monstrous-looking pocketknives have somewhere from 10 to 20 blades. The larger kit is more complex and uncomfortable to use. Now you might ask why it has been designed this way.

Well, your pocketknife was initially designed as a utility knife. The producers did not deliberately make it for whittling or wood sculpting, for that matter. That's why the setting of the blade on your pocketknife matters. The closer it's to the middle, the better it's to handle it. Nonetheless, again, occasionally, all of it boils down to personal choice. Some people might work better if the knife is closer to the edge of the set.

Forming of the Blade

Sheepsfoot Blade

You must think about the shape of your blade. I advise the sheepsfoot blade shape. It's the one where the knife's tip is straightened with the sharp cutting side. The shape of the edge resembles the one for a bench knife or your run off the mill utility knife. It's a whole lot less complicated to sculpt and also cut out small details with the sheepsfoot.

On the other hand, plenty of pocketknives have a decrease tip shaped blade shape. It's the one where the tip is in the facility of the blade. It benefits general cutting functions; however, you'll discover it awkward if you're cutting timber generally. Naturally, you can always improve the blade using sandpaper and also a honing rock; however, that'll take a while and even some effort. If you have some crafty skills and also you can work with a mill after that, making use of that will certainly speed points up a little bit.

Lock Type

It's a feature of pocketknives as well as out fixed bladed whittling knives. There are various securing mechanisms for different pocketknives. Some lock the blade immediately when you turn it out; on the other hand, few have some sort of switch (like the safety on a gun) that you can flip with your thumb. Besides, there are those pocketknives that don't have any locks in all. No matter the lock kind, you must always remember to remain safe and also not close the knife on your fingers.

How to Choose a Whittling Knife

Possibly one of the essential whittling devices is a knife because, without it, we'd only have a little bit of un-carved wood. Although they could seem like straightforward devices, there are a lot of knives in the marketplace today, a few of which are good options for whittling and also others that are only used for other objectives.

If you're going to get a brand-new knife when you embark on a new whittling activity, below are some potential choices:

Opinel Carbon Steel Foldable: Everyday Carry Locking Swiss Army Knife is simple and also a sturdy tool. This folding Swiss army knife is a timeless selection for whittling as well as everyday work. Opinel carbon steel is tough and long-lasting, which suggests that it cuts well, withstands wear, and also is easy to hone. And also, every one of the Opinel knives is made with their signature Virobloc security ring to deal with the blade open while you're trimming.

Pros: Economical Durable blade that can be quickly sharpened, User-friendly blade lock

Disadvantages: Carbon steel blade wears away if wet.

Wood Making Sloyd Blade: This Sloyd timber sculpting knife includes a brief, sharp tip for delicate timber cutting and also precise job.

The top-notch carbon steel blade allows an excellent, straight cut through both soft as well as hardwood, which is fantastic from a whittler's viewpoint. And also, the ergonomically made handle is made from oak and massaged with linseed oil for less complicated grasp after hours of use.

Opinel Foldable Knife   Sloyd Knife

Morakniv Timber Making 106 Blade With Laminated Steel Blade, 3.2-Inch

The Morakniv Wood Making Blade is a precision trimming knife made in Sweden. With an ergonomic handle made from oiled birch, this is the sort of knife that feels great in your hand after hours of whittling. The knife likewise has a 3.2 inch long, robust, laminated steel handle, favored by greenwood workers around the globe.

Pros: Super resilient, laminated flooring steel blade Practical oiled birch handle and includes a sheath.

Morkaniv Whittling Knife

Flexcut Right-Handed Carvin' Jack

If you recognize that a tool isn't enough for all your timber sculpting as well as whittling demands, Flexcut Right-handed Carvin' Jack may be a multi-tool for you. This jackknife is made of 6 different Carving-specific edges and is developed for right-handed whittlers. It includes a sculpt, a Carving knife, a hook blade, a v-scorp, a gouge scorp, as well as a straight cut, which makes sure that you can finish every task.

Carvin' Jack   Whittling Jack

Flexcut JKN88 Whittling Jack, With 1-1/2 Inch tip Knife And 2-Inch Roughing Knife

If you desire the capacity to have several whittling tools but don't desire the weight, size, as well as the expense of a huge multi-tool, the Flexcut Whittling' Jack might be what you're trying to find. It's developed with two whittling-specific knives, including a 1.5-inch requirements knife and a 0.5-inch roughing blade.

Maintaining Your Knives

Now that we've discussed the information of whittling knives as well as a few of the very best knives you can obtain your hands on, we require to take a minute to recognize just how one is to take care of these devices. Remember that the quality of your devices compliments the level of ability you utilize.

The First Rule of Whittling

Currently, you'll hear this thing a great deal from me and all the various other whittling practitioners you will be familiar with. **If you wish to maintain your whittling experience as a reward, you need to keep your knives sharp as a daisy**. There's nothing even more annoying than a blunt knife and attempting to make it slash off and also cut through a piece of wood. It'll indeed occasionally resemble impossible. Well, anyway, the first concern is when do you recognize when it is due time to sharpen your whittling knife? Well, you'll realize it when it seems like it's getting more challenging and also harder to puncture wood. If your knife remains in tip-top shape and is sharp, then reducing, whittling, and shaping wood will undoubtedly feel like gliding your knife through butter-- well something like that. It certainly won't feel laborious. When your strokes start to feel hefty and you notice that you often tend to apply even more pressure into each stroke, then you understand that you need to hone your knife. Now, in the following area, we'll review the steps on how to sharpen your whittling knife.

Sharpening Your Whittling Knife

Note that there are lots of knife honing approaches that you can utilize. Some people will assume that their sharpening technique is the most effective one-- and that takes place a lot. Some would even advise one technique or device to prove it. Some also feel that the devices they advise are outright essentials. Nevertheless, it all just boils down to individual preference. You must understand now that the sharpening method I'll describe listed below is my recommended approach-- to make sure that you recognize.

The method you utilize to hone your knife will depend upon the sort of blade you're honing. There are various means to hone a world-class chef's knife, and of course, there is a different way to sharpen a whittling knife. The technique I'll share here is very standard, and also it'll undoubtedly be straightforward to comply with specifically for newbie. The best of all, I assure it functions well.

Let's start with the tools you'll certainly need.

Tools:

- Whetstone (i.e., a sharpening stone).

- Lubricating substance.

That's practically it-- that's all the devices you will need to sharpen your knife. Nonetheless, there are a couple of details that you ought to know. To begin with, when you enter into an equipment shop, as well as request a whetstone, the salesperson there may ask you what sort of sharpening stone you want to purchase.

Now, let's discuss diverse whetstone types.

Yes, there are various kinds of sharpening rocks-- don't ask me why I didn't design these things. For beginners, there are Japanese water rocks-- think about them as the thing that samurai warriors use to hone their blades. The extra expensive whetstones out there are the diamond-encrusted ones. And after that, there are honing rocks with varying degrees of grit as well as also various qualities. The ideal practice is to try multiple sharpening rocks and also see which one fits your requirements. If you're just beginning and are new to whittling, then you should buy a whetstone that isn't on the expensive side. Any ordinary sharpener that isn't costly will undoubtedly do. However, if using a genuinely pricey whittling knife, you don't want to use an el-cheapo sharpening rock on that. You don't intend to spoil a thoroughly excellent knife on an improperly made whetstone. Nevertheless, for the majority of blades, the typical $10 honing rock needs to work nicely.

So, what aboutwhetstone anatomy?

Yes, there are parts to your whetstone-- 2 of them. Notice that one side of your sharpening rock is harsh, and the other hand is excellent. One has fine grit as well as the various others have a harsh grit. Why's that? The response is straightforward-- the finer your grit, the sharper will undoubtedly be the blade that you sharpen on it. Nevertheless, you don't merely utilize the fine grit regularly. You generally start sharpening your knife on the rough sand; and afterward, you comply with that up by honing your blade on the fine grit.

Lubricants

Currently, there are a variety of lubricants that you can utilize to hone your knife. Well, why employ lubes in the first place? You make use of an oil to keep your blade cool while you hone it. You're primarily sliding the blade across a hard surface, which will undoubtedly raise the friction and also make the blade hot. Some blades get so warm that it warps, and you don't want to do that to a good knife. Lubricants also aid in removing the particles from your whetstone (likewise called swarf).

Well, you're grinding steel on a rock, so you should anticipate particles to find off, right? If you ask the specialists, they'll certainly advise that you utilize oil instead of water as a lubricant for your knife. Most of the individuals around will recommend mineral oil when honing a knife or a few other blades. So, suppose you're out in the wild as well as you neglected to bring your mineral oil. Should that quit you from honing your knife? Certainly not. As a little FYI, a lot of first sharpening stones won't need lubrication. You can just wash off the particles later on.

Steps to Sharpen a Whittling Knife

Now, what do you do after your knife becomes blunt after hours of practicing?

Get your devices all set. Now, the first thing you must do is to find out the harsh side of the stone with a finer grit.

Often it's evident, and all you have to do is to take a look at the rock.

Now, if you can't find the rough side, run a fingernail on each side, you can inform by scraping a nail on each side which side is smoother than the other.

1. Start with the rough side since you have recognized which side is the rougher of both, get your mineral oil (or some other lubricating substance), and pour some oil on the rough grit side of your honing rock.

   Don't be stingy; however, don't drench the thing either. You require enough to have the surface area lubricated-- not drenched. Now that you've prepped your honing stone, you prepare to sharpen your whittling knife.

2. View the angles
   The following action is to place the knife's blade versus the oiled whetstone. Now, before you begin moving as well as scuffing the blade versus the rock here's a little detail that you may miss out on however is rather crucial-- the angle of the blade versus the stone. Maintain a 10 to 15 level angle. It'll make your knife sharp enough for the majority of whittling tasks.

   It'll help if you preserved this angle while sliding your blade throughout the honing stone. If you have trouble doing that after that, you can buy a sharpening guide. The guide isn't truly that expensive (it's only 10 bucks), and also it can be a beneficial financial investment, especially if you're intending on acquiring a costly knife.

   Sharpening an item of metal isn't rocket science. All you require is a sharpening surface (i.e., the

   sharpening stone or whetstone).

   Again, the lube aids in cleaning the surface area and also lowers the temperature.

   To hone a blade, what you're truly doing is getting rid of some product off of the blade's side, so that you'll undoubtedly end up with a sharp as well as the clean side. To remove that material, you must use a reduced friction movement, which avoids producing too much heat.

   3. Start the process with the narrow end facing you. Hold the knife with your right hand. The sharp edge of the knife's blade needs to be encountering far from you. Elevate the level edge of the knife up until you make a 10 to 15-degree angle.

The sharp side of the blade should keep in contact with the whetstone.

You can utilize your left hand to hold the blade stable, assisting in maintaining the angle, or you can utilize that hand to maintain the sharpening rock steady.

Currently, while keeping that angle, slide the blade ahead, scraping the surface of the sharpening rock when your blade is nearing the back of the whetstone, angle the blade a little bit to make sure that the tip of the knife type of meets the corner of the whetstone.

Lift the knife and placed it back to beginning placement (i.e., at the end of the honing stone that's close to you).

Repeat the same stroke. Do it overall frequently. Now, don't put excessive stress when you grind the blade's sharp side against the sharpening rock. You recognize that you're overdoing it when you hear an awful screeching sound. What you should be listening to instead is a nice scuffing sound.

Push in or swipe away?

Now there will be those who will certainly say that pushing the sharp edge of a knife towards the stone won't work.

They'll essentially disagree with this part of my approach right here. What they'll likely advise is that you swipe the blade away and not towards the sharpening stone.

Well, honestly, I assume it's just an issue of preference-- yet once more. You see, I've tried both directions-- cutting right into the whetstone and swiping away from it-- and you understand what I discovered: both ways function.

Doing that generally makes your sharpening work a great deal a lot more reliable.

4.   Repeat

So, you do it around once more. Place the blade back on one end of the prepped side of the sharpening stone. Raise the blunt end to the desired angle. Grind the sharp end versus the whetstone. When you get to finishing the stone angle or turn the blade a little bit so that the suggestion of the blade fulfills the edge (or somewhere close to it) of the whetstone. Do that ten times on one side of the blade. Repeat the same process on the other side of your knife's blade.

5. Finishing touches

To finish things off, turn the sharpening rock over as well as put sufficient oil in addition to the rock. This moment you're most likely to work using the fine grit of the whetstone.

All you have to do is to duplicate the same process explained steps 3 and 4. Grind the blade of your blade versus the stone on one side about 10 times and afterward do the opposite side of the blade.

Later, you're done.

Using a Handheld Sharpener

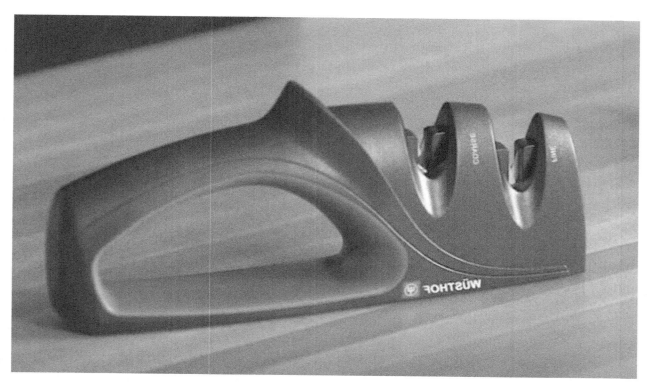

As specified earlier, the huge problem is keeping the angle of your blade against the honing rock.

If you can keep it at 10 degrees, then you can be sure that your knife will certainly remain very sharp. Nevertheless, with handheld sharpening, you can't always preserve that angle, right? That's why manufacturers have invented what's called a handheld sharpener.

It has a much better handle as well as a more natural grasp. Remember that there are two slots on this handheld sharpener. It functions virtually the same way as your sharpening stone. One of the positions on this handheld is the great side (i.e., great grit), and also the other is the coarse side (i.e., rough grit).

The advantage of this tool is that the positions already preserve the angle of the blade. That indicates there's no need to adjust any kind of angles. There's no second-guessing involved.

Currently, see the follow to ascertain exactly how you make use of a handheld sharpening device:

- First off, hold the grasp with one and then hold your knife with the other.

- Put the knife's heel near the sharpener's handle (i.e., your hands need to be close together).
- Next, draw the knife blade back with the position from the blade's heel to the tip. You need to hear a great and also grind audio created by your blade running against the sharpener's slot.
- Repeat these steps up to 5 times.

Now, make use of the fine side or grit of the handheld sharpener for blade upkeep-- which will certainly have to do with every 2 hours of whittling work. Now, if your blade has dulled out, you simply do the same thing as you would certainly do with a whetstone.

You'll initially grind your steel blade on the rough grit (i.e., the coarse slot) 5 times. Afterward, to complete things off, run the blade through the finer side of your handheld sharpener-- and afterward, you're done. That's exactly how very easy it is to utilize this device. The only drawback to it is that it's a bit large, which means you'll certainly need to make space for it in your set or bag when you go outdoors.

Whittling Knife Maintenance and Storage

Your whittling knife is one of the most crucial tools you'll certainly ever use in whittling. That's why you should not only know just how to sharpen it-- you ought to likewise know just how to take good care of your whittler. Whittling knives are made use of by Do It Yourself (DIY) crafters as well as true blue woodworkers. Even survivalists will advise that people should have a pocketknife on them. Your whittling knife can be utilized for a variety of different applications, especially when calamity strikes or when you're outdoors. You do not just use it for sculpting. You can likewise use it for cutting rope, digging, making holes, and of course, for safeguarding yourself. In this area of this publication, we'll review the general upkeep steps to expand the functional life of your whittling knife.

Use your knife just for its intended objective.

You'll eventually own different knives. Some knives will be made use of in the kitchen area.

Power knives are more of a general function kind of knife-- something that you use to puncture anything like cardboard, wood, rope, etc. A whittling knife naturally needs just to be used for whittling. A general function knife can get curved as well as deformed in various methods when you use it for other applications. Some even make use of knives as screwdrivers. Doing that can damage the tip of your knife, so take care. The best method is that you should just utilize your whittler for whittling, and nothing else. Use your other knives for other things. And you additionally don't want to use your pricey cook's knife for anything but cutting and pre-whittling lunch. The same regulations apply.

Sharpening Your Whittling knife

We've already discussed the essentials on how to sharpen your whittling knife in the earlier discussion. Simply remember that you ought to go lazy on sharpening your whittling knife and that there are various honing devices that you can use, including the following:

1. Stone Sharpener: This is the one we have covered in the product earlier. It has two sides-- one with a rough side and also a fine side. There are natural stone sharpeners, and there are those that have little rubies on them. Different producers use various types of abrasives when building their whetstones.

2. Handheld Sharpener: This is the other sharpeners that I described above. It has positions on it and manages to keep things steady. The main advantage of this sharpening tool is the truth that it has taken care of slots, which suggests your blades are sharpened perfectly at a 10 level angle. No more uncertainty in contrast to by hand grinding your blade versus a whetstone in liberty.

3. Electric Sharpener: These sharpeners are somewhat comparable to handheld sharpeners just that they are device powered. It's, without a doubt, the fastest and most efficient method to hone your whittling knife. All you have to do is to set it, mount the knife, and push the switch. If you're always in a hurry, then you can buy one of these home appliances.

Stropping your blade

Homemade Leather Strops

After you have sharpened your knife's blade, you ought to check it to make certain that it is sharp. You recognize that your knife is ready when you feel across the blade as well as the side feels smooth as well as straight. On top of that, you'll certainly feel that there are little bits of sand at the edge. Those are burrs, and you need to strop your blade when you discover those. Discovering burrs on the edge of your knife likewise suggests that your blade has reached its sharpest point. All you need currently is to remove the burrs. You do that by stropping your blade-- to do that; you swipe each side of your blade across the size of a natural leather strap, which you can purchase from an equipment shop.

After stropping the sharp edge, check the blade once more for burrs. If you discover that they have been removed, then you're done. If you still feel a couple of bits of sand-like things along the side, after that duplicate the procedure. You'll recognize that you're done stropping when the blade acquires a specific luster.

Clean as well as oil your blades.

Don't forget to hone, tidy, and also lube your blades after usage. Yep, if you don't have time, then avoid sharpening for later, but don't ever forget to tidy and also oil your blade. You should clean up the blade, rotates, and manage. There must be no timber bits or little pieces left in your knife-- you'll be amazed to find them in the most unusual spots. To clean your knife, hold it under running water-- get it damp yet don't get it soaked. Afterward, you ought to dry your knife extensively. Make sure that all wetness has been removed; otherwise, it can cause the steel and also other components to wear away. Currently, keep in mind that you need to never place your whittling knives in the dishwasher. It'll certainly leave your knife in the water more and also rust and corrosion can accumulate quickly. If you notice any type of staining on the knife's blade, then it means corrosion has begun, so clean your knife immediately. You additionally need to lube your knife blade with oil from time to time to avoid rust development. To get it done, all you needto do is to add a couple of drops of oil on the blade and afterward spread the oil along the length of the blade with a clean cloth.

Knife Storage Space

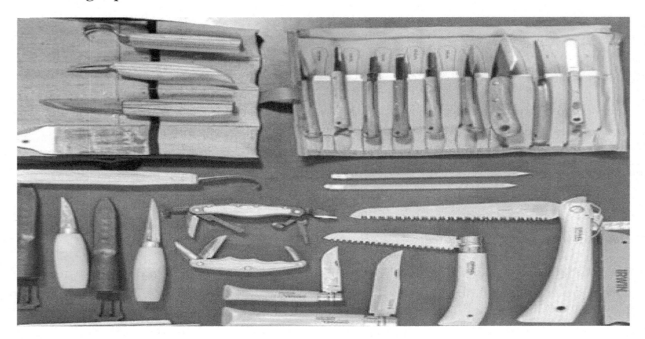

Different Knives

To maintain your knives, you ought to store them properly. Proper storage space also keeps you (and even the kids) secure. The sort of storage space you pick is all approximately you. There are magnetic strips that you can set up on the wall where you can keep your knives and various other devices (like screwdrivers, saws, etc.) far from the reach of kids. One more option is to keep your knives in a tool kit as well as maintain it secured to make sure that children cannot get to them. Keep the toolbox in your workshop as well as out of the reach of your little ones. When keeping your knife in a box or toolkit, you need to place it in a safety sleeve as well as, not just a sheath. The sleeve secures the blade from damages as well as it likewise shields your browsing hands when you reach inside package sensation for a tool you require. Now that you recognize exactly how to sharpen and also look after your whittling knives, we're most likely to go over how to utilize them. We'll cover the basic whittling strokes in the next chapter.

Workspace with Knife storage

4. Techniques of Whittling

When you consider whittling, you may visualize an older man on a front porch in a shaking chair with wood shavings spread at his feet. Yet, whittling is a leisure activity that covers generations, genders, as well as skill levels. With unwinding activities and also meditative effects, every day, brand-new individuals are joining the art of whittling. Whether you're a devoted carver or merely curious about woodworking, below are some whittling techniques and tips to bear in mind.

Wood

Soft straight-grained woods are preferred for whittling as well as carving. You're advised to prevent making use of wood with knots, as they can be challenging to carve. Basswood is among the most typical novice woods to work with, but pine, aspen, and also balsa are also excellent options. You can locate wood for whittling at your regional craft shop or sculpting supply shop.

Grain

Grain describes the development lines or the pattern of the wood fibers. Recognizing grain is a crucial element of whittling, as well as something you'll intend to take notice of as you make your cuts. We always try to cut the wood in the direction of the grain. If you discover your wood shavings are crinkling, this is a good indication that you're cutting in the ideal instructions.

Basic Cuts

- **Straight Cut**--This cut is done while forming the wood piece and gives you the general form /structure of the wood piece.

- **Pull Cut**-This is the same cut we do while peeling a potato. Also known as a thumb cut, it's used majorly during whittling.

- **Sweeping Cut**-Pushing it in and away: This cut isn't like sharpening the stick. It's more controlled with the help of the thumb and usually used at the edges or corners. For example, see below, as it's used for making a hat.

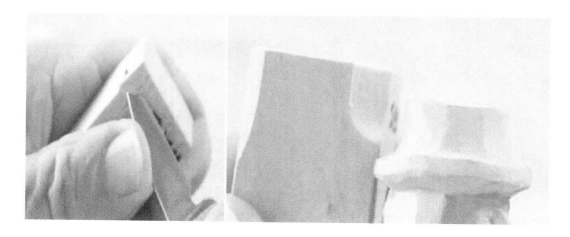

- **V-Cut**-- This cut is terrific for including detail to your wood, typically made use of when developing the look. The V-Cut is also helpful when cutting unique lines to differentiate functions. Cut at 45 degrees from both sides to make a perfect V cut.

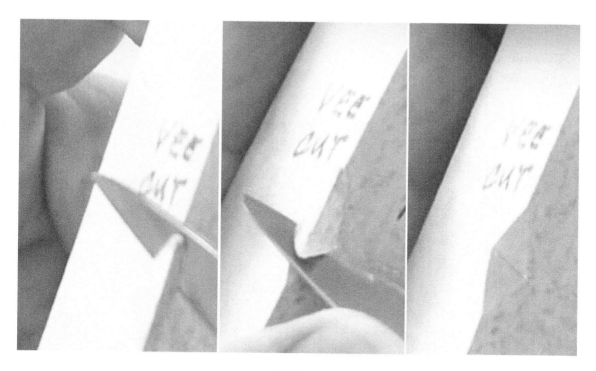

V Cut

- **Stop Cut**

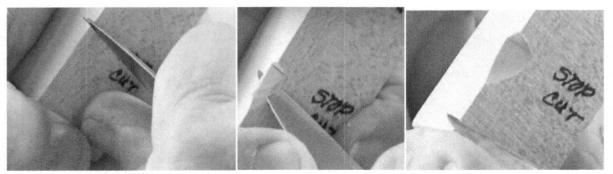

So this cut comprises three steps, as shown in the pictures above:

- Make a straight cut.
- Take the push action below it until the cut and stop (Come up to it).
- Remove the wood.

Cut in and come up to it. A stop cut makes the bottom of a nose or hat.

- **Pyramid Cut**

This cut looks like a triangle or pyramid. Your handgrip should be a pencil grip for this cut.

Holding the knife

Before we start with whittling, let's discuss holding the knife properly.

In case you're right-handed, your left hand should hold the piece of wood, and the right hand should hold the knife. The left thumb should be on the back of the blade, as well as will be offering the cutting force. Never press the blade ahead with your right-hand; you won't be able to move the blade with precision.

Notice that the fingers should run out the path of the blade.

Don't be silly:

Never push hard on the blade. If it's stuck (since you carved too deep right into the wood or the grain positioning changed), quit as well as backtrack. If you attempt to force the blade, it might slip and also cut your finger.

There's no demand to go fast. Rate doesn't aid you to carve better. Take your time until you feel comfortable.

Listen:

The noise, as well as the feeling of your cuts, is essential. You can listen to the distinction between Carving with, against, as well as across the grain. It'll undoubtedly be useful in establishing instinct concerning the direction you're cutting in.

Technique

So let's figure out what occurs when you carve: You'll be making a scooping activity. First, the knife needs to dig into the surface area of the wood a little. The knife needs to be then pushed through the wood; it's all about the angle!

As you push with the wood, angle the knife up, and you will undoubtedly have slashed off a little bit of wood. With lots of wood, the shavings will crinkle; this is an indicator that you're entering the appropriate direction.

You must eliminate the wood in skinny layers; if you go deep, you'll end up tearing out your en route backup.

A great way to learn knife control is to attempt keeping the knife handle at an advised angle; see how long of cutting you can make in one cut. The more you carve, the more you'll recognize the grain. It's rather tough to explain in a paragraph with a few images. However, it'll certainly make sense as you experience it first-hand. Start with delicately curving objects that enable you some space to make mistakes. As you get better, add details regardless of the orientation of the grain; there's always a method to make the right cut. Most importantly, have fun all the way.

5. Safety Tools and Instructions

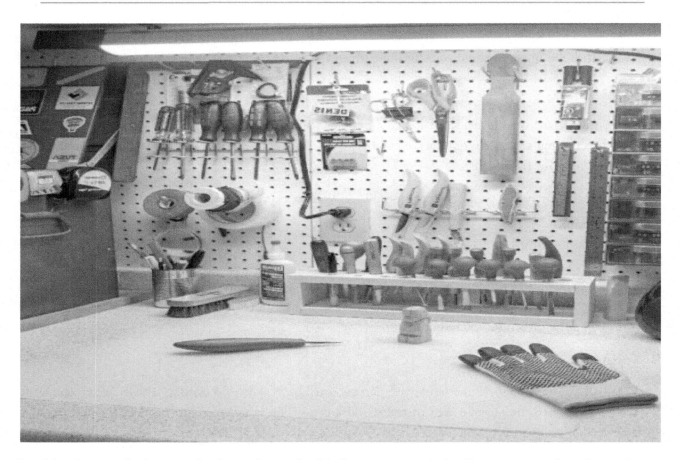

In this chapter, before we look at the real whittling projects, let's discuss a couple of security reminders and also basic guidelines.

Safety is essential whether you're whittling a stick in a park or when you're servicing a precut block adhering to a cutting pattern.

While starting, don't be overconfident with the knives and rigidly follow the below suggestions:

Work with Your Project Slowly

During my first whittling project, I was in a hurry to complete it as soon as possible. However, rushing didn't give me the outcomes that I was anticipating. Things have altered ever since.

My first little bit of safety and security recommendations are to function slowly.

Keep in mind that whittling is something that you can do to pass the time.

That indicates hurrying to finish a job isn't the way to go. I know that there are whittling jobs that can be carried out quickly, as you can see videos on YouTube about finishing simple whittling projects in a few minutes. However, there's no reason for attempting to make your whittle that quickly-- especially if you're starting.

Take time to try out the cuts. Concentrate on understanding the fundamental strokes first. Opt for far better knife control instead of making speed cuts.

Precision, as well as efficient cuts, are your main problems when you're starting. Keeping a sharp edge, I recommend honing your whittling knife before you work on your task as well as additionally after you've finished a project.

If you're working on a longer project, I suggest that you hone your knife every 1 to 2 hours of use. Use the fine side of your sharpening stone or tool for sharpening.

In this way, you don't eliminate any metal of your knife's blade to preserve its edge.

Keep in mind that maintaining your knife sharp is a safety and security precaution too. A sharp knife will certainly bite into the wood rather than slip and possibly cut your hand.

Bear in mind: sharpen your blades before and also after use as much as possible.

Place on a Pair of Cut Resistant Gloves

I've tried various sorts of hand wear covers all these years.

Whether you're starting or experienced, there are chances that the knife would slip, causing blood stains all over. The gloves can prevent that for sure.

So, which work hand wear covers are best for whittling?

Selecting a glove is always up to your budget and liking. Let me explain my experience with different types of gloves.

Leather hand wear offers you theright level of protection, yet they sometimes hinder your hands, thus making them much less maneuverable. Some leather gloves are rigid, but some are softer; however, I doubt if they can supply you with sufficient security from a sharp blade in the long run.

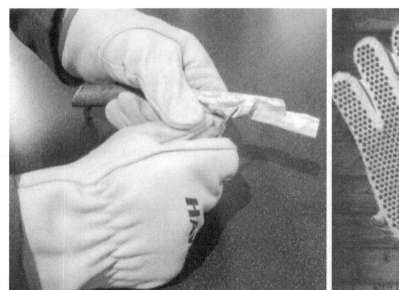 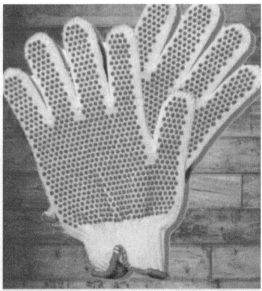

My Collection of Gloves

Now, I additionally received a pair of job gloves that are made from DuPont Kevlar. Well, these Kevlar gloves that I saw weren't made explicitly for whittling on wood, but they were perfect.

Your hands stay maneuverable, given that they are soft, and an additional plus is a truth that they're super lightweight. It's made by G & F items. It's the G & F 1670L as well as it's not that costly (less than $10). It's not a one size fits all, so I don't know if it'll fit a young person's hands. However, hey, anything to keep your hands from getting bloodied will be excellent. On top of that, these hand wear covers are truly tough, so expect them to last a while.

Thumb Guards or Thumb Pads

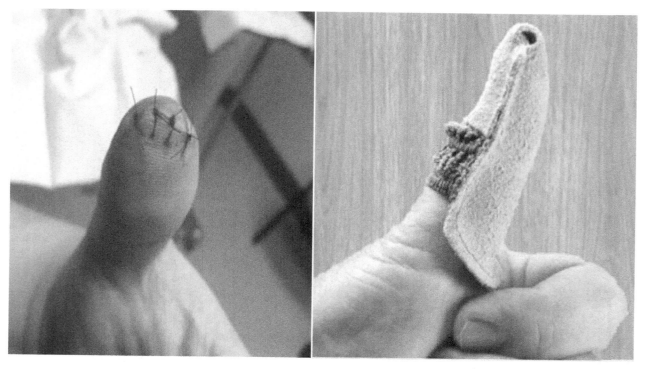

If you do not use safety gear   Thumb Guard

Now, if you don't feel comfy wearing gloves, as well as you choose to have the feeling of timber in your hands, then the next best thing you can do is to put on a thumb guard. You use a thumb guard or thumb pad on your knife holding hand considering that it obtains the burden of all the nicks and also cuts. Currently, a thumb guard is different from a thimble-- yeah, the one you use when you knit and stitch. Although I've seen some experts who utilize thimbles when they do whittling work, well, there are plastic thimbles and metal thimbles.

Yet I seriously question that it can offer you full defense when you're dealing with a pocketknife. It's just not big sufficient. Sure, it covers the point of your thumb; however, there are various other parts where on your finger where your blade can cut you.

A thumb guard is undoubtedly bigger, and it covers the entire length of your thumb as it should. Thumb guards are different one from the other. Some are made from thick elastic fabric, while others are made from split natural leather. Some are made from a mix of both. You take your pick. They're also cost-effective-- around seven dollars or less (I assume there are thumb pads that are sold for less than two bucks). They're further usually sold in sets, so you can wear one in each of your thumbs-- lefty or not, there's one for you.

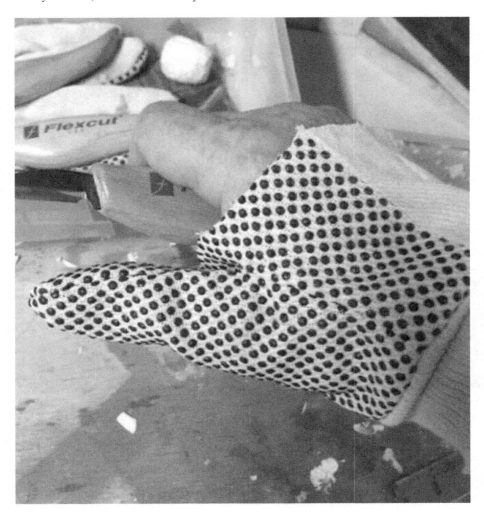

Thumb guard made out of gloves

Good Old Air Duct Tape (or Whittlers Tape - if you like)

Now, thumb pads, as well as gloves, ultimately worn out.

So, what do you do when your own get worn, and also you don't have time to drive to the store to obtain a brand-new set?

It can likewise happen when you're out in the woods or when you're camping, and your hand wear cover slits or your thumb guard crumbles-- so what do you do?

Like every outdoors type would advise, you must always bring with you a roll of air duct tape. Yep, this is going all the way economical on this but pay attention-- it functions. Note that there's a whittler's tape or carver's tape sold in woodcarvingshops and also craft shops, which are about the same price.

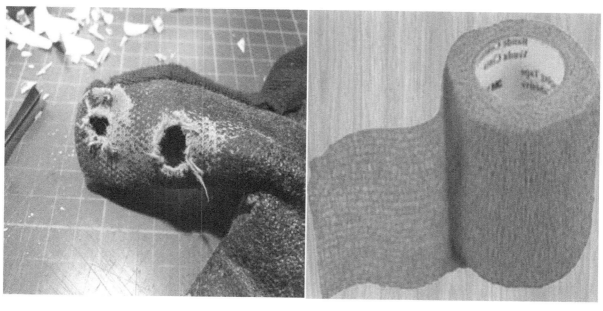

Worn out Gloves   Carvers Finger Wrap

You can cover duct tape (or carver's tape) around your thumb to work as a short-lived (or in some instances semi-permanent lower temporary) thumb guard or thumb pad. You can go gung ho and cover the thing around your thumb as well as have the time of your life attempting to remove it later (it's sticky, keep in mind?) or do what I do:

- First, you should wrap air duct tape around your thumb with the sticky side dealing with outward-- yes encountering outside. By doing this, the sticky side doesn't stick on your thumb and also give you a tough time later when you're done whittling.
- Wrap it around your thumb tight enough, so it doesn't slip off easily. Nonetheless, don't

wrap it too tight that it makes your thumb lose blood flow and make it feel numb. One layer is all you require.

- Next, cover an additional layer of air duct tape around your thumb, yet this time around the sticky side, please deal with the internal.
- Ultimately wrap one more layer or 2 of air duct tape also with the sticky side encountering internal.

With several layers of duct tape on your thumb, you have a proper thumb pad on. It's cheap as well as additionally multiple-use (that is if you don't fail to remember where you tossed it). Now, if you feel that your air duct tape layers seem like they're as well slim to stop a sharp blade, then add two or three more layers if you desire. It's all up to you!

6. Starter Projects

Owl: One of my favorite initial projects

Project 1: Christmas Tree

Tools Required:

- Whittling knife
- Saw
- Paint for decoration (optional).
- Branch, diameter 3-4 cm (1.25 - 1.5 in) or completely dry lime wood (basswood) 1 x 3 centimeters (0.5 x 1.25 in).

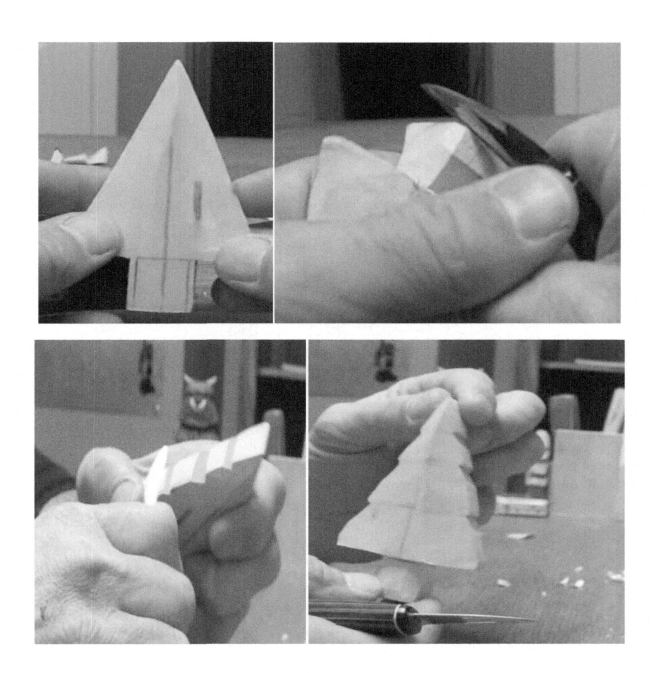

Steps involved:

Basic Whittling Process

- Hold the wood with one hand as well as the knife with the other.
- Make sweeping cuts away from you along the grain of the wood - this is an excellent method for lengthy cuts. You won't always have the knife entirely in control when using this technique, so take care.
- While sitting, splay your legs or flex them away, so you don't cut into them.
- Lean the knife slightly laterally; this offers you the most effective cutting technique.

The Thumb Push Process

- This technique is suitable for thorough and regulated wood carvings.
- Press the thumb of the hand holding wood against the blunt side of the blade to press as well as direct the knife forward.
- At the same time, relocate the knife somewhat up and down. Your thumb might obtain aching, to begin with, so stick a plaster over it initially!
- This method is used for cutting into wood or if you aimto make a groove.
- Don't neglect to transform the job when essential, so you're always whittling away from your body.

Exactly How to Make Your Fir Tree

- Whittle, a point, then narrow two opposite sides for the grooves. You can make use of an axe to approximately form your tree initially.
- Sculpt grooves along the sides - take care the tips don't break off.
- Saw the tree to the proper length. (Cut by saw)
- You can repaint or enhance your tree, if desired.

Project 2: Smiling Spirits

Tools Required:

- Whittling knife
- Pencil
- Strop
- Triangular wooden block (ideally Basswood)

Pencil, Triangular Block, and Knife

Steps Involved

- Taper Down the sharp corners
- Stop cut in the middle for carving the bottom of the nose of the spirit.
- Also, make another cut 1 cm above the middle cut.
- Taper up until the center cut, as shown in figure 4.
- Make a similar v-shaped cut 1 cm above center-cut, where we have marked in step 3.
- Now the side view would be like a nose.
- Mark the centerline with a pencil.
- Mark the nose line with a pencil and apply a stop cut along the line.
- Make another stop cut in the perpendicular direction for theeye socket.
- Remove the wood from the eye socket.
- Mark the nose and again apply stop cut to carve out the nose.
- Sharpen the nose and then make a straight cut to carve the forehead.
- Make a similar cut below the nose to make a mouth.
- Draw a smiling line and make a stop cut on the line.
- Make push cuts from below to the nose to get rid of the wooden chip below the nose.
- Draw the lip with a pencil and cut along the lip with the tip of the knife.
- Carve the eye.
- Make the hair and the beard. First, mark the lines with a pencil and then apply cuts through the knife.

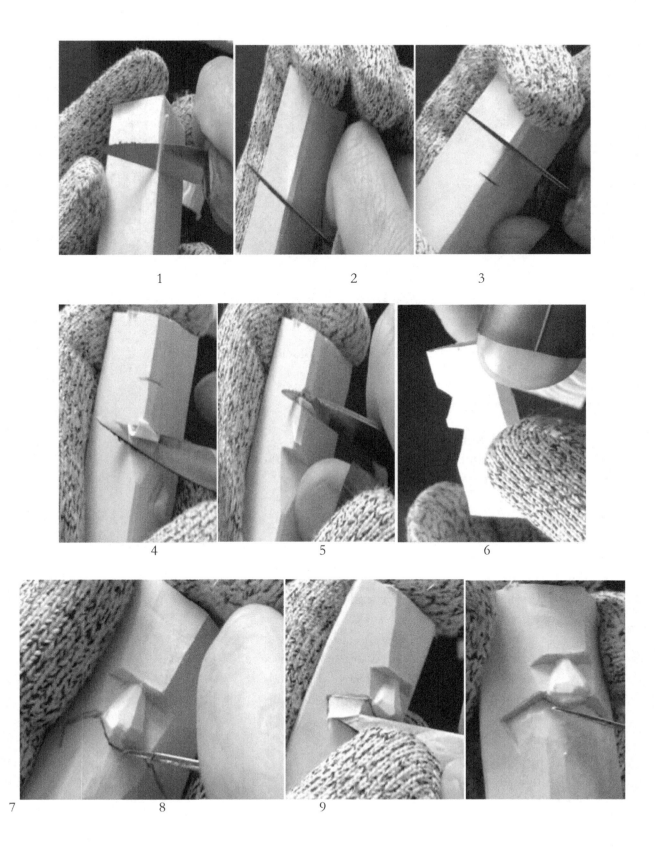

1   2   3

4   5   6

7   8   9

68

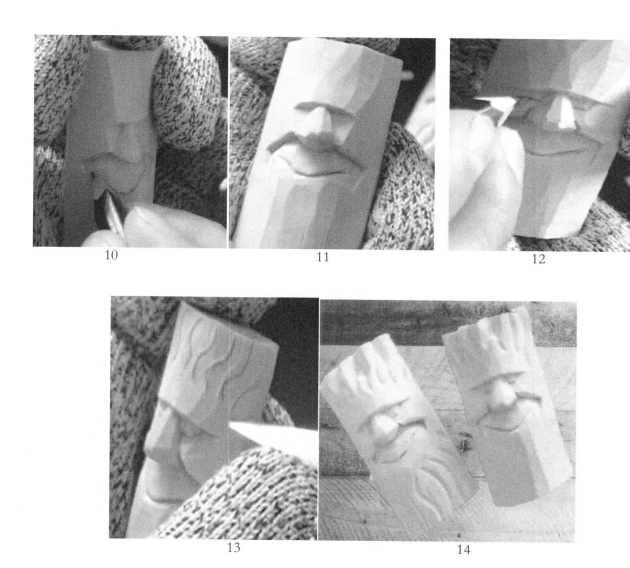

10   11   12

13   14

Project 3: Chess Pawn

Tools Required:

- Whittling knife
- Saw
- Strop
- Wooden Stick

Steps Involved

- Remove the Bark.
- For making the round head, apply push cuts from the bottom of the thumb.
- Make a pencil line on the wood below the head for stop cutting.
- You can also have this stick held up against your chest and just cut toward yourself, maintaining a fair distance away from your fingers. You'll likely be tempted to take quite big chunks off the wood. Our experience is that it actually works a lot better and if you just make little small bits.

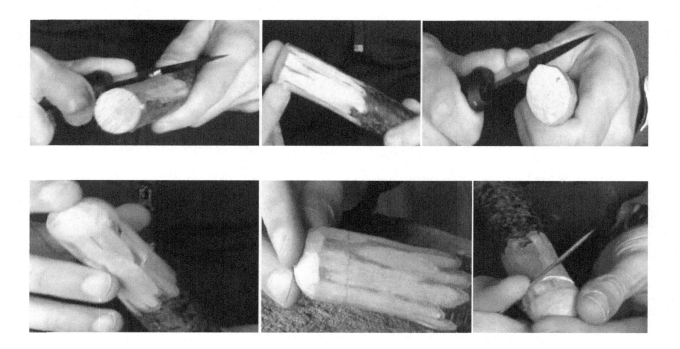

- After getting the round head, make one more cutline about quarter inches below the first line, as shown below.

- Apply push cut from below to the cut line above, as illustrated below.

- This push cut would give a slanted look to the bottom part of the chess pawn. See the rightmost picture below.

- Just cut the rest of the stick with a saw. Here's your chess pawn.

Project 4: Bonfire Fork

This fork is a handy camping accessory.

Tools Required:

- Whittling knife
- Wooden Stick (around 3/4 inch wide and length as per your comfort)
- Strop
- Sand Paper

Steps Involved

- Mark the handle with a V-groove: Pick how much length to make the handgrip based upon what fits for you. Add a V-shaped groove that notes where your handgrip ends, and the shaft begins.

- Make the shaft part flat: Both top and bottom parts should be trimmed so that the shaft is flattened somewhat. Do this by holding the handle and carve away from yourself.

- Bend the sides of the shaft: Cut the sides and curve them somewhat. It aids to leave the completion intact to ensure that you understand you aren't cutting into the entire stick and only the middle part of the shaft.

- Make the Tip sharp: Sharpen/Hone the pointer to ensure that it is shaped like a flat-head screwdriver. Ensure you cut down the top and also bottom, as well as avoiding the sides.

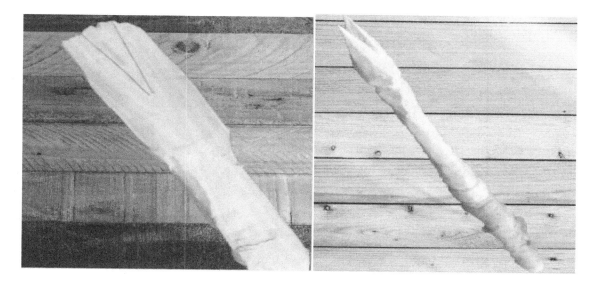

- Make the prongs: Make the prongs by whittling your cuts and afterward going all the way through with your blade. You can have two or three prongs.

- Sanding as well as Outlining: Outline your fork. Simply make V-grooves as well as continue shaping the fork. Once the outlining is done, you can sand; if you like the 'harsh' look, don't sand.

Project 5: Horse Chess Piece

Tools Required:

- Whittling knife
- Saw
- Strop
- Wooden Stick

**While reviewing the projects, let me remind you that we use softwood, wet wood, and a sharp knife. Also wear protective gloves.

Steps Involved
- Take a suitable wooden piece
- Square the wood.
- Depending on the dimension of your horse, cut the wood to size. It could be 1-inch thick and 2 1/2 inches high.
- Now taper the sides up, from about midway up the 'log.'
- Tamper the leading to make a triangle form. It'll be the horse's head.
- Make v cut for the ears of the horse.

- The most challenging part is making the horse's neck. Here we need to make sloping cuts.

- I 'd advise eliminating all the bark from the front of the horse, from halfway up, like the tapered sides, just not as deep. You're just attempting to do away with the bark.

- Then start the neck. It'll take several cuts. Don't utilize hardwood for this task, because it could slide off as well as cut your hand.

- First, make; sloping under-cut. On this cut, you're not managing any wood; you're just cutting.

Two types of horse chess piece

- The 2nd cut must squeeze off the wood, connecting to the previous cut.

- By doing this, you'll slowly dig a little hole under the horse's head, gradually making the jaw/neck. Beware when doing the undercut, because you might slice off the horse's nose.

Project 6: Egg

Keep in mind: Whittling an egg usually is risk-free. It can quickly be done without cutting yourself. Never cut toward your hand or fingers and continuously make use of a sharp knife if your hands get tired, quit, and rest them.

Tools Required:
- Whittling knife
- Strop
- Wood: 2 1/2 inch wood piece with a thickness of 1 1/2 inches
- Safety gear – Gloves or Thumb guard
- Sandpaper
- Pencil

Steps Involved

- The first step is finding the right wood piece. You can also look for a scrap wood at construction sites.

- For your first egg project, you can take a wood piece of size 1 1/2" x 1 1/2" x 2". It will provide you a great sized egg that does not also take longer to carve.

- Cut a scrap of wood into a shape in which the length and size, are even. Also, the deepness is somewhat longer (about a 3rd longer or width times 1.33).

- If you don't have a saw for this objective, I presume you know someone that does as well as might enjoy assisting.

- Cut both the ends into a round shape. Carve away the edges to make it cylindrical. Mark a line at the center to signify the widest part of the egg. See the followingpictures.

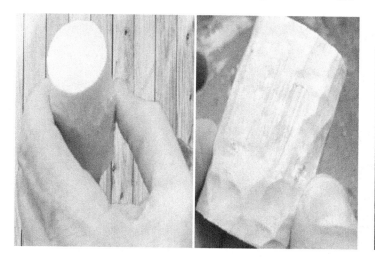 

- Chip the cylindrical wood to make it egg-shaped, as shown below.

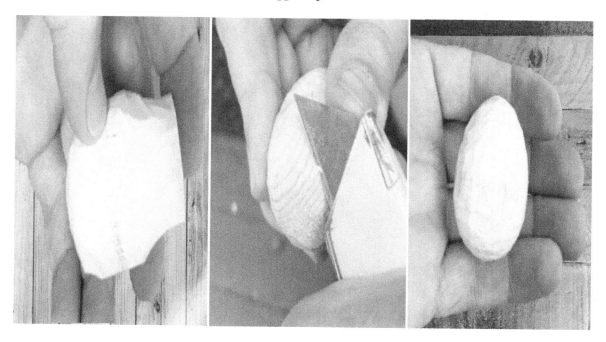

- As a next step, you can take the sandpaper as well as begin raveling all the peaks. Starting with rough paper to cut faster (regarding 100 grit) and afterward use finer grit paper to achieve the level of smoothness preferred.
- You can then use the finishing coat on the egg by using paint, oil, clear coat, marker, etc.

Project 7: Mushroom

Tools Required:

- Whittling knife
- Strop
- Wooden Stick
- Wooden cube for Carving

Steps Involved

- Take the wooden piece and mark the top view of the mushroom (spherical).
- Mark the side view with the mushroom structure.

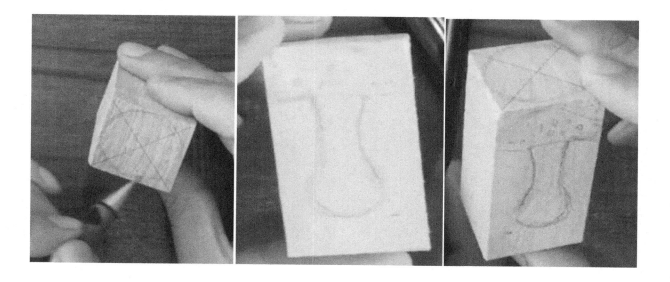

- Apply push cuts from all sides at the top to make it circular.(Head of the mushroom)
- After that, mark a deep cut on the circular head of the mushroom below which the stem of the mushroom is to be carved out.
- Apply push cuts from the bottom too top to make slant stem off the mushroom.
- Further shape the mushroom head.

- Make the mushroom leg thinner by applying upward cut from bottom to the cut line of the head.
- Give the final touches by making the head and stem below more prominent.

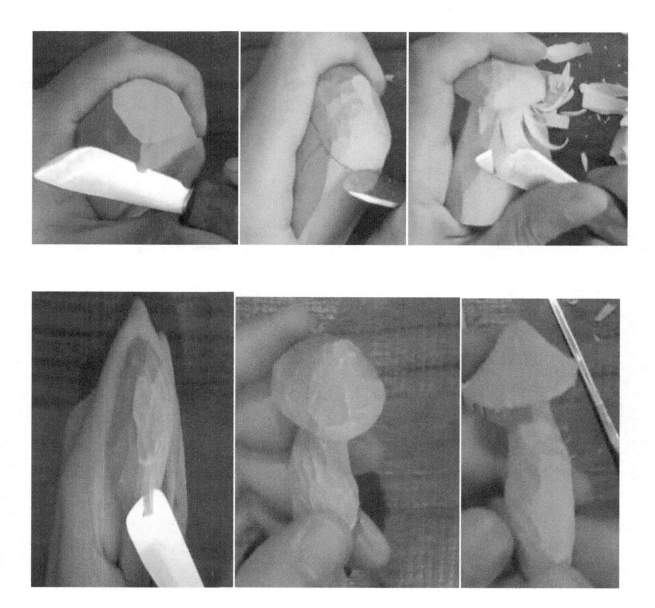

Project 8: Wooden Spoon

Tools Required:
- Whittling knife
- Strop
- Pencil
- Wood piece – 6 x 1 x 1 inches.
- Spoon gouge or curved knife
- Sandpaper with 120, 180, and 320 grit
- Axe

Tip: Choose a softwood

Steps Involved

- Choose the wood piece where the grains are running straight. See the below picture of a wood piece.
- Remove the bark from the wood piece.

- Draw the spoon figure on the wood piece.
- Chop the sides /edges from top to bottom to make the handle thin, as shown below.
- Draw another line around the circular scoop of the spoon for marking the thickness of it.
- Take out the spoon gouge or curved knife and make the scooping motion to dig out the depth in the spoon, as depicted below.

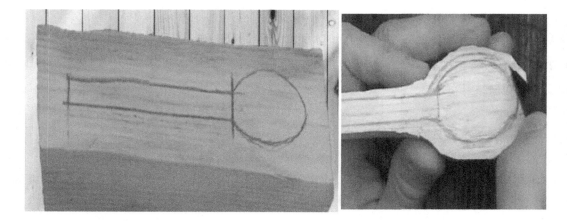

- Now remove all the excess wood around the handle from all sides.
- Lastly, sand it down to a smoother surface and apply finishing oil /paint, if required.

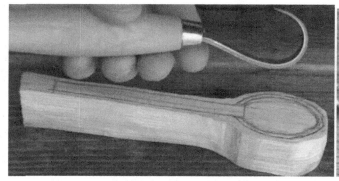

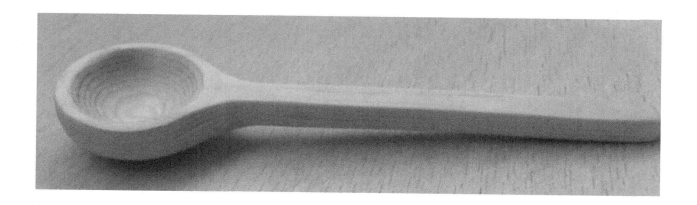

Project 9: Forest Spirit

Tools Required:

- Whittling knife
- Strop
- Wooden piece
- Pencil or pen

Steps Involved

- Draw the face on the wooden piece.
- We're using the tip of the knife to mark the line with it. Carve at the head using stop cut, as shown below.
- Carve out the eyes.

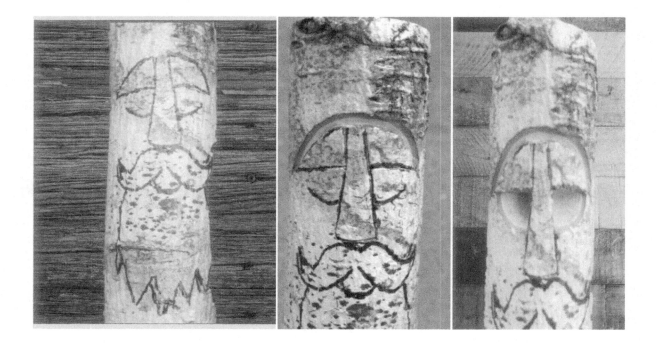

- Peel off the bark to make a face like skin.
- Carve Cheek Bone.
- Peel off the eyebrow and nose.
- Peel off the moustache and beard.

- And you're officially done. The eyebrows, moustache, and beard are dark brown because just the bark is peeled off.

Project 10: Wooden Boat

Tools Required:

- Whittling knife
- Strop
- Pine Bark
- Pencil or pen
- Hand Saw
- Straight Chisel

Steps Involved

- Use saw to remove the bark and make it triangular
- Use a whittling knife to remove the leftover bark and give it boat shape, as shown in the figure below

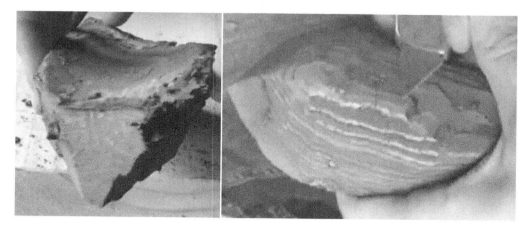

- Draw a straight line and use an axe to cut the extra length
- Chip off the excess wood to give the base of the boat below shape.
- Start with marking a line on the top of the boat. Then the wood to be chipped away to give depth on the top of the boat using a chisel and a knife.

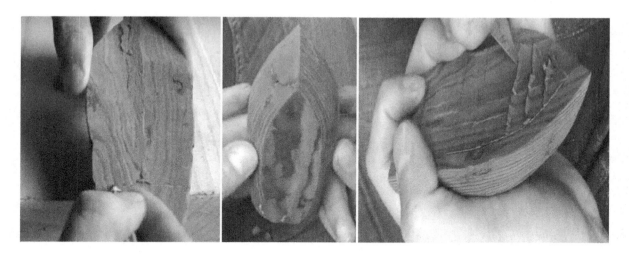

- Continue Carving as per the design, leaving a straight line in between two grooves/holes, as illustrated below.

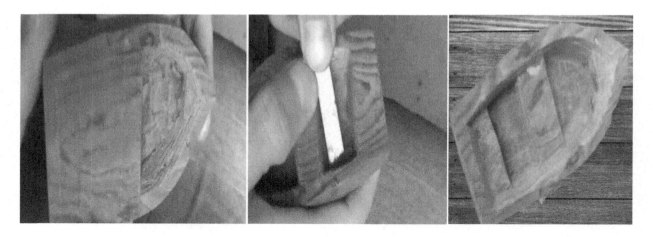

Project 11: Wizard

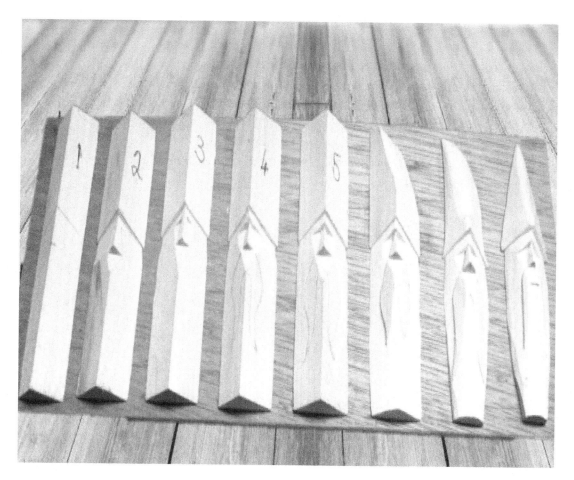

- Whittling knife
- Pencil
- Strop
- wooden block (ideally Basswood)

Steps Involved

- Make a stop cut for making the bottom of the nose.
- Add a flat triangular surface with a nose as a center and carve out eyes.
- Draw moustache and carve out the surface around moustache on the same level as a triangular face carved above.
- Now the moustache looks exalted above the surface around it.
- Make the cap above triangular-shaped by using the sweeping cut.
- You cans and it and color it.

Project 12: Hook Pendant

Tools Required:

- Whittling knife
- Strop
- Pencil or pen
- Coping Saw
- Wood
- Flaxseed oil

Steps Involved

- Draw the pendant with a pencil on the edge of the wood.
- Use the coping saw to make a hole from the top inside the hook, as revealedin the below figure.
- Apply sweeping cut on the edges around the pendant, as shown in the third figure below.

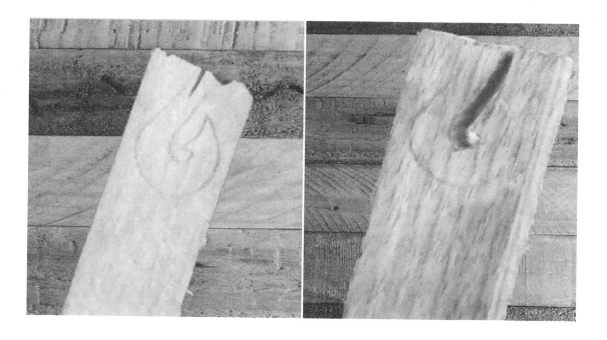

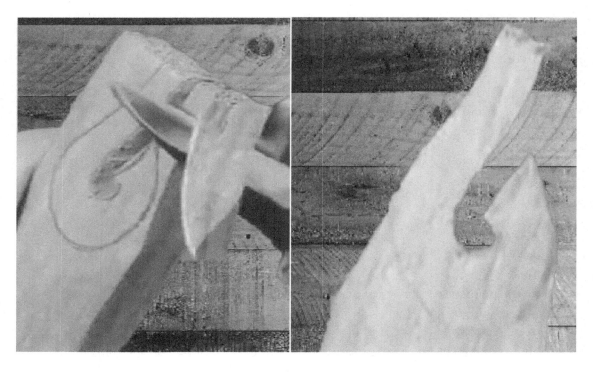

- Draw the pendant with a pencil on the edge of the wood.
- After shaping the pendant from all sides, apply a stop cut at the inner side of the pendant to give it teeth form as shown below.
- Cut the wood below.

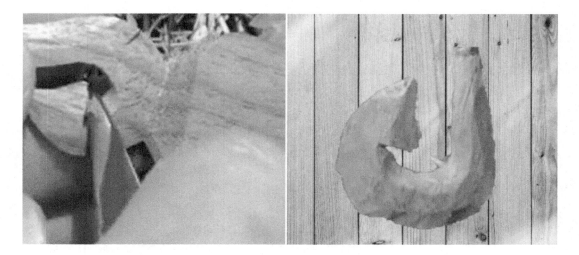

- Apply the linseed oil for finishing.

Project 13: Heart

Tools Required:

- Whittling knife
- Strop
- Pencil or pen
- Coping Saw
- Wood (Preferably Bass wood)
- Flaxseed oil

Steps Involved
- Draw the heart on the piece of the wood.

- Cut along the heart line with a saw.

- Use push cuts to shape the heart, as demonstrated below.
- Remove the handle and make the heart more sharp by using a whittling cut.

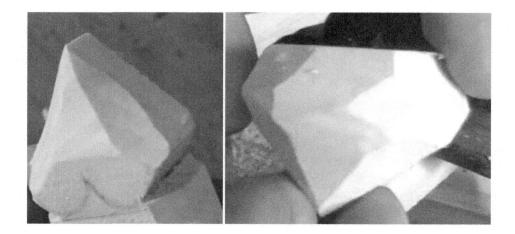

- Smooth the heart with the cut against the thumb, as shown below.
- Make a V cut at the top center and deepen from both sides, as shown below.
- Dip in linseed oil to finish it.
- Take out the heart from the oil and clean off the extra oil with a cotton cloth or paper.

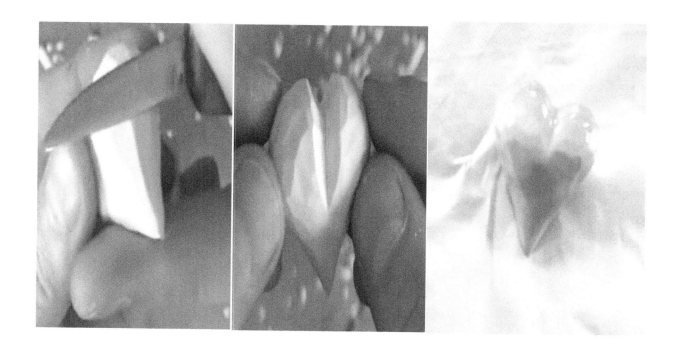

Project 14: Birdie

Tools Required:

- Whittling knife
- Strop
- Pencil or pen
- Pattern
- Wood (Preferably Basswood)
- Sandpaper
- Beeswax

Steps Involved

- Cut out bird pattern. 4 pieces: up, down, left, and right.
- Stick these four patterns to the four sides of the basswood.

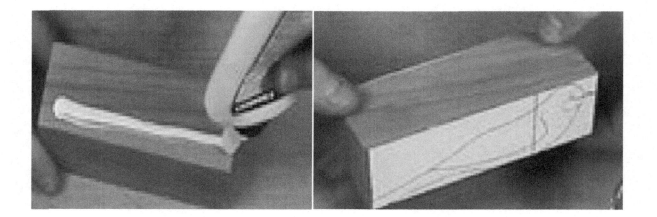

- Cut the wood along the lines, as per the pattern stuck on the four sides.
- Keep whittling until it resembles the below shape of a bird from all the sides.
- Sand the bird with sandpaper.
- Finish with beeswax.

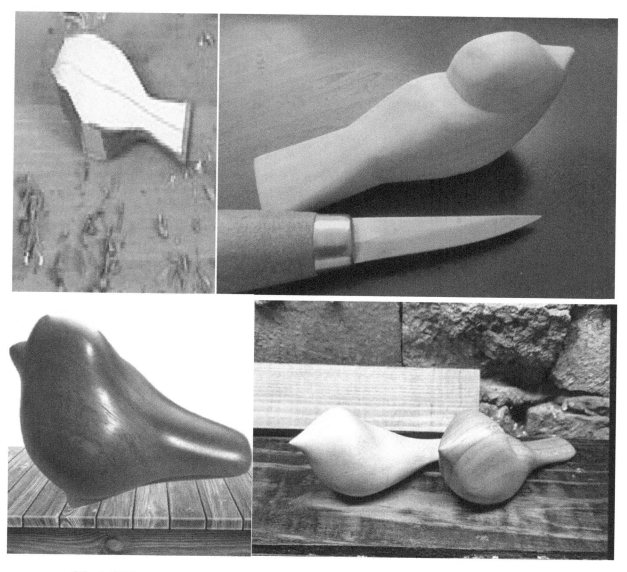

Black Walnut   Pine and Sapele

- Above is the comfort bird made out of different woods like Black Walnut, Pine, and Sapele after finishing.

7. FAQs from Practitioners

These are the few questions/issues I've encountered during my whittling career while interacting with other fellow crafters.

They aren't in particular order, but I'm jotting them down as I remember them.

The answers are the suggestions we received during various discussions in the classes from the people who had the same issues and how they resolved them. Therefore, there may be different solutions to a single problem. I'd suggest you try all the solutions and follow the one best suited for your environment. Remember: The best solution is the one which works for you!

1. **Question about custom fitting knives. If a person is big (Large Palm Size) and any available knife doesn't fit his/her hands or feel comfortable, what's the rule of thumb to help people determine the optimal grip thickness and shape of a Carving knife?**

   Below are the various suggestions on the above problem:

   - Get a chunk of wood. Carve at it until it feels good. Or, pick up all kinds of tools until you find one you like. Most smiths and even some factories will make custom handles.

   - You can buy just the blades and carve your handle to fit your hand/style of carving.

   - You can always wrap a handle with surgical, electrical, duct, or even masking tape and contour it the way you need it.

   - The only rule of thumb regarding handle size and shape is what you feel comfortable using.

2. **I want to buy a spoon Carving knife and possibly a carving jack and can't decide whether or not I need a left or right-handed blade.**

   - You can always turn your woodblock upside down. And then pick the right hand. Because of the other tools on the knife, right-handed would be my choice.

3. **How do I know if the wood piece is totally dry?**

- A moisture meter is helpful, but only to the depth of penetration. Moisture slowly weeps out of the wood. The surface can be fairly dry while the core is still very wet. The denser the wood, the longer it takes to dry.

4. **I just got a pocketknife as well as some wood the other day. I've never done anything crafty before in my life. Was just wondering the very best way to sharpen a little pocketknife? All the cuts I've done are very messy; I'm attempting to whittle a little guy.**

- You can use a whetstone with oil as well as a strop. Beware with folding knives; they can slip and cut your hand while sharpening.

5. **What's the purpose of the curved cutting edge in the below knife?**

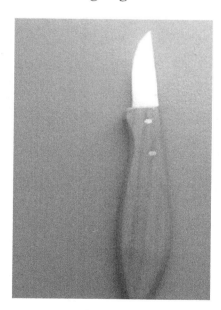

- A curved edge works best when smoothing out deeper cuts. Being right-handed, it gives me much better control over the exact angle of my cut in the wood. You can use this knife like a bevel down chisel with about a 15-degree angle.

6. What's the difference regarding carving between white pine & yellow pine?

- I believe yellow pine is the hardest of the pines. I've seen it in houses for floor covering.

- White pine is a softer, typically extra usable, finer-grained wood than yellow pine. Yellow pine is often rough, and the darker grain is harder than lighter grain.

- Yellow has more resin pockets and is tougher to get a tidy Carving.

7. I make use of a cut-resistant glove on my left hand. I'm looking for a suggestion on thumb protector and padding when utilizing my right-hand.

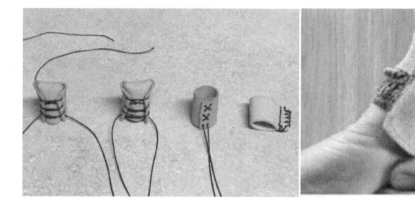

Home Made Leather Finger protector   Thumb Protector

- Online sites sell finger protectors out of the same knit material as the cut resistant gloves.

- You can use an old bicycle inner tube cut to size of your thumb and padding.

- You can also use the thumb off a pair of old leather gloves.

- Cut the fingers off a right-handed cut glove, and you got five thumb guards.

- You can make your own from the vet-wrap animal bandage

8. What sort of paint are you utilizing on your finished pieces?

- You can use acrylics and a spray sealer. We often paint, spray, and then use an antiquing medium to highlight the Carving. (You paint it on, then wipe off, leaving it in the crevices.) You follow with a few more coats.

- If you want the color to be more transparent (more like a stain), you can use watercolors or dilute acrylics. Just practice on scraps or projects you discarded, so you can learn how they travel in carved lines, etc. For solid colors you can touch up, but if you want the wood grain to show through, there's little room for error.

9. Suggest a few YouTube channels for beginners?

Below are the ones I came across and were suggested by experienced crafters:

- Doug Linker
- Gene Messer
- SharonMyART
- DougOutside
- Kevin Coats
- Eric Owens
- Lynn O. Doughty
- SticksandstonesCarving
- Gary McDaniel
- Dan Cuomo (Rick Butz videos)
- carverswoodshop
- MrSplinters

10. I plan on getting a strop. Which one do you suggest for a beginner, and also will I also need some stones for further sharpening my whittling knives?

- For sharpening, we use the Flexcut strip with Flexcut gold paste.

- When a knife is just not cutting smoothly, run it over a right hard Arkansas stone that's well furnished and in good condition for excellent sharpening.

- Good Arkansas stones take practice to get the hang of, and time to burnish and develop extremely fine sharpening. Which knives you use will determine what other stones you might need.

- We have Flexcut knives that never seem to need anything more than stropping to stay sharp. I have pocket knives that regularly need touching upon a true hard Arkansas stone to maintain right whittling edges. I have a Rick Butz roughy, our knife that regularly needs to be brought back to life using a soft Arkansas stone or a 1000 grit diamond stone. You'll have to learn your knives to determine what they need.

- As a warning tip—if you don't have experience sharpening knife edges, I would strongly recommend getting some. Get yourself a soft and hard Arkansas stone set and a couple of old pocket knives that don't mean a whole lot to you and learn how the stones work and what it feels and sounds like to get sharp, and then refine and polish a good edge.

- I recommend Arkansas stones because they're inexpensive, readily available at most outdoor shops, and do an excellent job of sharpening and polishing an edge, both of which are very important to safe and efficient whittling.

11. How do you refurbish a leather strop after metal and polishing compounds accumulate over it?

- Use the edge of a tri square and scrape the buildup off the strop.

12. Are the carvingblade covers of knives made in 2 pieces and gluing together?

- They're two pieces with the blade shape carved out. They're usually wrapped in leather.

- You can make small blade covers from leather. Cut, glue the edges with contact glue, wait untiltouch they're dry, fold over, compress, punch holes,& stitch.

13. **Can you share some websites where I can get a pattern and idea for a new project like sea animals?**

- There is a turtle project at the Woodworker Institute. Below is the link to it.

https://www.woodworkersinstitute.com/wood-Carving/projects/animal-Carving/reptiles/mock-turtle

14. **What's spaltingon a block of wood, and how does the project result with that type of wood?**

- It's where a fungus caused the wood to stain. It actually makesfor a beautiful piece when finished and sealed properly.

- The finishing will likely bring out more contrasts and deliver an exciting piece.

- Appreciate the beauty of nature and roll with it. It's all good and should bring a better price than a plain old piece of wood. In woodturning, people cultivate these cultures and intentionally spalt wood for these effects.

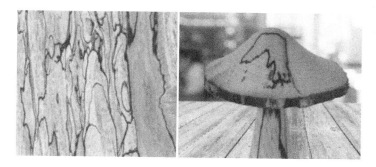

15. **After you paint your carving, do you seal them with anything?**

- Wrong order. Always seal the wood before you paint it.

- Seal, paint with water-based paints (from the local dollar store), and then final coat water-based varathane.

16. **Why don't some tools like Pfeil spoon knife come pre-sharpened?**

- The reason is the bevel. Not all carvers like the same bevel on their tools.
- I like a 20, but some prefer a 10,and so on, so this way you're free to put your bevel on for your style.

17. How to sharpen a spoon carver knife?

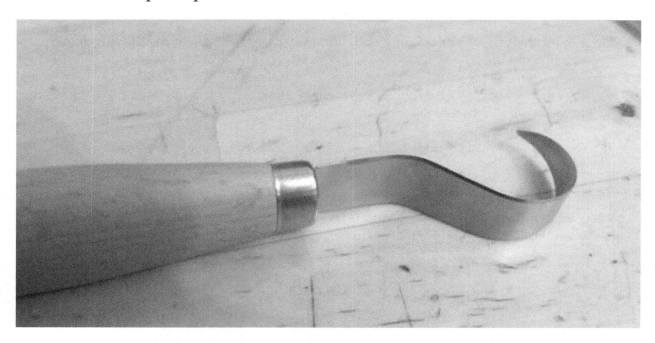

- You can have some sharpening sticks for hook knives that helped me. More information can be found from YouTube is HuronSpoonCo.

- Wet and dry paper wrapped around a piece of round wooden dowel, then do the same with some leather and stropping compound.

18. I've heard about soaking harder woods in an alcohol-water mixture to help soften the wood. Share your views and experiences. Also, will the wood crack after drying?

Below are the experiences shared by fellow crafters:

- I'd bought some basswood eggs online, and they were super hard. Once I did the soak for maybe 5-10 minutes, but it was like cutting butter. It didn't take long at all.

- Wet and dry paper wrapped around a piece of round wooden dowel, and then do the same with some leather and stropping compound.

- I've had no adverse effects from soaking the wood for four days, carving on it, and letting it dry out. No cracking in the wood was found.

- Reference Video on Youtube: The Alcohol Water Solution for Hard Wood- Gene Messer

So, my take on the above is that the solution (only water or mixed with alcohol) and the time frame (a few minutes, hours, days) depends on the wood type and size. The perfect timing only happens by experience.

19. I started whittling after watching a few YouTube Videos (Doug Linker and Gene Messer). But the real work is tougher than how simple it looks in videos. I'm now discouraged after a few attempts. How do I go about it?

- It takes years to master a craft; one way to never master art is to get discouraged. Give it time to keep trying. Watching videos is good, but remember, these experts have been doing this for many years. Don't be too hard on yourself; you'll learn from every piece you work on. Great crafters are always willing to help. Just remember when you ask 10 carvers how to do something, you'll probably get 10 different answers, and they may all be correct.

- The most common mistakes I see are blunt knives (watch some YouTube on sharpening) and expect to cut away too much wood (gently, slowly, take it easy. You can cut away too much, but you can't cut away too little)

- Do yourself a favor and buy some Flexcut pre-sharpened knives and gouges. They're razor sharp. Use Basswood to start instead of hardwoods. Also, have a hand and thumb guard. You'll be good to go!

20. When trying to take or shave off a layer off basswood, more often than not I get wood

splintering, usually more than I need to shave off. It also creates an ugly pattern that needs to be shaved even more. What's an excellent technique to avoid that?

- Cut in the opposite direction, with the grain. Think of the grain-like petting a cat. When you pet it head to tail, the fur all lies down, and the cat purrs. If you try to go from tail to head, it spikes up, and the cat gets very angry. Keep the cat happy (This analogy isn't mine, one master crafter told me).

- You also might try spraying it with a 50/50 mix of rubbing alcohol and water. Your wood might be too dry. Keep your tools sharp.

21. What are the best suggestions for coating my dog project made of Basswood?

- You can use Tung oil and wipe on polyurethane. And sometimes, mix a semi to medium darkness of stain with the oil.

- Beeswax 1 part and mineral oil 3 parts. Creates a low gloss natural coating

- Most things you add to wood will darken its melamine lacquer. In sum, the best I've found that doesn't darken it or give it a yellow color.

22. For someone young and beginning the whittling journey, what are the tips for keeping the workspace clean?

- Regarding cleaning the mess and keeping your house tidy: If you carve with a knife, the mess is easy enough to clean up. Sit in a chair and put an apron on to help catch the chips. The chips can besweptup.

- If you have a plastic dishpan/basin, you can set that on your lap to catch the chips, too. If you show your parents that you're willing to clean up after yourself, maybe they can be swayed. I wouldn't sand or power carvein the house, but just a knife makes a very manageable mess.

- You can use one of the big reusable shopping bags on the floor in front of me and vacuumup the mess.

8. Free Whittling Patterns

1. Go to Foxchapelpublishing and download free issues.It contains one free pattern.

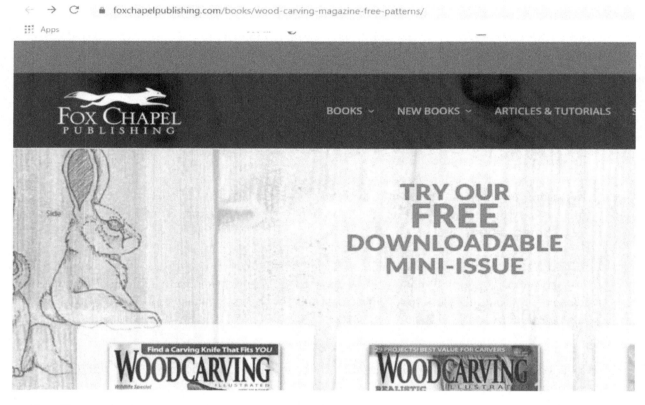

2. Pinterest is one of the best place to find free patterns

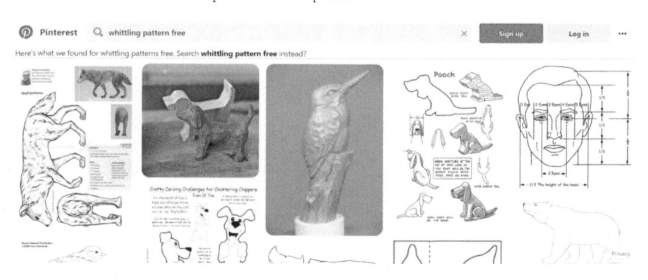

3. Central Texas Woodcarvers website has got many categories of patterns available

https://www.centraltexaswoodcarvers.com/

centraltexaswoodcarvers.com/Woodcarving%20Patterns.html

Patterns	simultaneously press the keys CTRL and + to increase, or CTRL and - to reduce; or 2) on a Mac simultaneously press the keys Command and + to increase, or Command and - to reduce.
Woodcarving Tips	
Members	
Woodcarving Galleries	
Newsletters	
Links	
Contact	

In the Round Woodcarving Patterns

Bear

Dogs

Armadillo

Small Bird

Whittlepup

Buzzard

Gecko

Giraffe

Mother Goddess

Wren

Crucifix

Mouse

Alligator

Cat

4. Jemome.com- 12 Photos of Easy Whittling Patterns

http://www.jemome.com/p-easy-Whittling-patterns-2233620/

ⓘ Not secure | jemome.com/p-easy-whittling-patterns-2233620/

> Use strong, geometric typeface to reinforce your message.
> Do not use a distinctive icon and the symbol that you see everywhere to represent your topic.

5. The Woodcarvers cabin: Duck Decoy Pattern and Process

http://www.thewoodcarverscabin.com/workshop/how-to-make-a-duck-decoy/

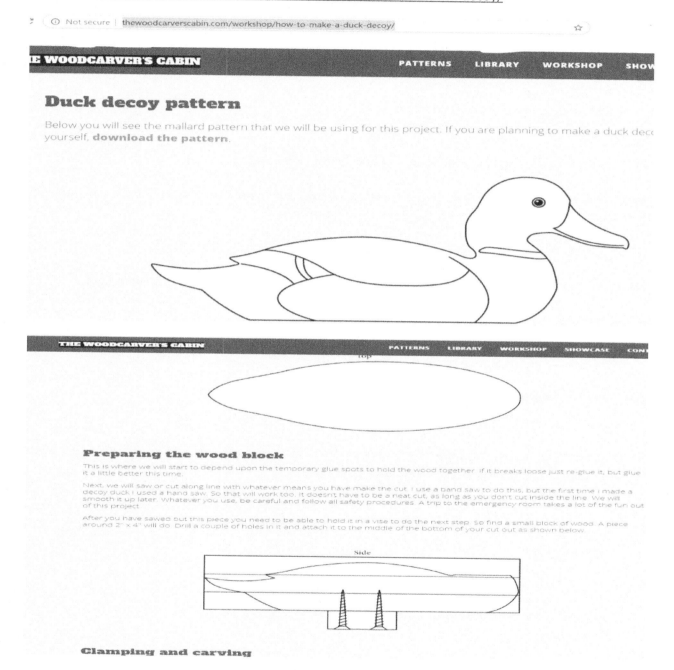

THE WOODCARVER'S CABIN   PATTERNS   LIBRARY   WORKSHOP   SHOW

Duck decoy pattern

Below you will see the mallard pattern that we will be using for this project. If you are planning to make a duck deco yourself, **download the pattern**.

THE WOODCARVER'S CABIN   PATTERNS   LIBRARY   WORKSHOP   SHOWCASE   CON

Top

Preparing the wood block

This is where we will start to depend upon the temporary glue spots to hold the wood together. If it breaks loose just re-glue it, but glue it a little better this time.

Next, we will saw or cut along line with whatever means you have make the cut. I use a band saw to do this, but the first time I made a decoy duck I used a hand saw. So that will work too. It doesn't have to be a neat cut, as long as you don't cut inside the line. We will smooth it up later. Whatever you use, be careful and follow all safety procedures. A trip to the emergency room takes a lot of the fun out of this project.

After you have sawed out this piece you need to be able to hold it in a vise to do the next step. So find a small block of wood. A piece around 2" x 4" will do. Drill a couple of holes in it and attach it to the middle of the bottom of your cut out as shown below.

Side

Clamping and carving

9. Conclusion

Whittling is all about freedom.

You can choose:

- Where you want to whittle
- How much time you would like to take
- What shape you want to whittle

There is no set rule, and everyone is free to use their imagination.

This sense of freedom and creativity separates Whittling from other similar crafts. Probably early whittlers started this art form with the same thought process.

So what next!

Take out your favorite knife, go for a hike, pick up a piece of wood, and start the whittling!

Here's wishing you the best for your first project!

Cheers,

Stephen Fleming

(If you liked the book, kindly leave a review. In case you want any improvement or to share something, please email me at valueadd2life@gmail.com.)

My Other Books

Book Link or

https://www.amazon.com/gp/product/B083XGJSV4

TOP 500 REVIEWER

5.0 out of 5 stars Want to Try Leatherworking? Start Here

Reviewed in the United States on February 9, 2020

Format: Kindle Edition

If you've ever had an interest in learning how to do leatherworking, this is the book to get you started. As the author states in the book description as well as within the book itself, he has not been doing leatherworker for long—about 5 years—but he seeks to fill what he sees as a gap in the market, one that he found himself when he was just learning. Namely, as he wanted to learn the craft himself, he discovered that there weren't modern leatherworking books geared toward the true beginner. Books were often old, about projects only, or assumed the reader would already know particular techniques. He set out to make this book so that you could use it to begin your exploration of this hobby, learning about tools and techniques. The book is full of information that the rank beginner would need to know, shared by someone who has obviously been a beginner himself not that long ago. If this topic interests you at all, check out this book.I received a free copy of this book, but that did not affect my review.

Book Link: <u>Click Here</u>

Or <u>https://www.amazon.com/gp/product/B084Z13PBJ</u>

VINE VOICE

5.0 out of 5 stars Very complete instructional.

Reviewed in the United States on February 20, 2020

Format: Kindle Edition

Not long ago I purchased a wood-burning kit. Many years ago I had worked this craft the only problem was that I could not find any books with tips. When I saw this one on Booksprout I knew I had to download. This book had everything I was looking for from the type of burner, to how to hold, from protection and cleaning this book had it all. I loved the project ideas and the patterns were great. I cannot wait to try the Easter eggs. This is a very complete book and will give a newbie or someone who has forgotten most of what they knew the leg up they need. I highly recommend this one. I did receive a free copy of this book and voluntarily chose to review it.

Made in the USA
Columbia, SC
15 December 2021

51581852R00063